Preface

Space! No, not the futuristic 'Final Frontier' sort of space, Trekkies can deal with that while Neil and I concentrate on the past – a warm cosy place with light, colour, coffee, egg and chips, and, once, the Gloster Meteor.

'Space' refers instead as how best to allocate it. FlightCraft 11 EE Lightning, included about 160 archive photos which, given the type's production run of just 339 airframes, still presented a challenge in including as many relevant and interesting photos of the Lightning as possible within the space available. But total Meteor production ran to *eleven* times that figure, approximately 3880 airframes in all, thus, with the same amount of space available as before, how best to include yet more photographs? Hence our decision to restrict coverage to Meteors in British service and to replace large elements of body text with comprehensive tables listing Meteor squadrons, Marks used, when, and for how long. A *select* listing of other British units relevant to the Meteor is also provided. Surprisingly, by economising in this way, sufficient space then remained to allow us to contradict the book title by including a full-colour glimpse of some of the Meteors once operated by the *Centre d'Essais en Vol* (CEV) in France.

Given the importance of the Meteor it is hardly surprising that its development and service history has been thoroughly documented by many publishers over the years – however, for today's reader who wishes to acquire a more detailed understanding of the subject we heartily recommend Volume One of Roger Lindsay's seminal *'Cold War Shield – RAF Fighter Squadrons 1950-1960 – Spitfire, Tempest, Hornet, Mosquito and Meteor Squadrons'*, as well as *'Gloster Meteor-Britain's Celebrated First Generation Jet'* by Phil Butler and Tony Buttler.

Authors' note

In 1947, Arabic numerals replaced Roman-style numbers, thus the Meteor F.III became the F.3. For simplicity's sake, Arabic numerals are used here throughout, which will upset the purist, but is intended purely to avoid unnecessary duplication given that early Marks served through the transitional period.

Acknowledgements

The authors would like to express their sincere thanks and gratitude to Tony Buttler, Francis Chapman, Rick Greenwood, Roger Lindsay, Fred Martin, Huw Morgan, Bill Newton and Terry Patrick, for their much-appreciated assistance in connection with this project. Our gratitude is further extended to Mike Smith and the staff at Newark Air Museum who helped enormously yet again. Of course, we always mention our good friend Mark Gauntlet who has truly excelled himself once again, not just with regard to the quality of his superb illustrations, but his research too – it was Mark who found the archive film footage of EE455 confirming it wasn't quite the all-yellow Meteor many enthusiasts are accustomed to thinking of.

F.8, WH453 from 5 CAACU seen on 5 May 1971. Apparently coded 'L' at this stage, it certainly carried that letter in later years as a D.16. *Newark Air Museum*

The Gloster F.9/40

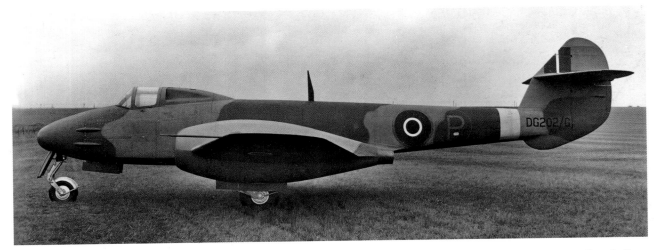

Designed by the Gloster Aircraft Company (GAC), their new jet became the first to enter squadron service with the RAF as well as the first British jet fighter to fly.

GAC was issued with an order to produce twelve prototype F.9/40s in February 1941 with serial numbers DG202 to DG213, although in the event only the first eight were ever completed. Because of the importance and secrecy of these new aircraft each had the suffix 'G' added to its serial to signify 'Guard', i.e. unless they were in the air then they were to be guarded at all times.

Between them the F.9/40s tested various jet engines from different manufacturers and it was DG206/G which became the first to fly. Respective first flights occurred in the following sequence: DG206 (5.3.43); DG205 (12.6.43 crashed 27.4.44); DG202 (24.7.43 – disregarding a 'ground hop' on 10.7.42); DG203 (9.11.43); DG204 (13.11.43 – crashed 4.1.44); DG208 (20.1.44); DG209 (18.4.44); DG207 (24.7.45).

Top: Gloster F.9/40, DG202/G, was the first of type, but not the first to fly. Seen here in its original form, it was fitted with narrow-piped Rover W.2B/23 engines and lacked an 'acorn' fairing on the leading edge of the fin – although one was in place by mid-August 1943. The pilot's original field of view aft was severely limited, being restricted to two vertical transparencies in the rear of the cockpit with recesses on either side of the rear fairing. By mid-August 1945, DG202 had received a sideways-opening canopy. *Tony Buttler collection*

Centre: Having survived and its significance recognised after serving as a gate guardian at Yatesbury, DG202 was restored, albeit not quite to its original form. Seen during the 1960s, the error concerns its camouflage, whereby DG202/G was repainted Dark Green and Dark Earth when in fact it was originally painted Dark Green and Ocean Grey with all-yellow undersides and a Sky rear-fuselage band. As far as we know it never received a coat of Dark Earth! *Author's collection*

Bottom: Viewed from certain angles F.9/40, DG204/G was, in the author's view, one of the most pleasing members of the Meteor family to look at by virtue of the underslung MetroVick F.2 engines, which required some modification to the undercarriage. DG204/G was painted Dark Green and Ocean Grey with all-yellow undersides but did not receive a Sky fuselage band. *Via Tony Buttler*

Top: This image of DG204/G reveals that a fin-mounted acorn fairing had been fitted prior to its crash on 4 January 1944. Also evident are the underslung engine nacelles, its lengthened undercarriage, nose-wheel strut and door. *Newark Air Museum*

Left: Amongst other duties, DG205/G was used for flight control development. Its first flight was on 12 June 1943 with Michael Daunt at the controls. This image predates August 1943 when this airframe received an acorn i.e. bullet fairing. Left to right are: John Crosby-Warren (who was killed when DG205/G crashed on 27 April 1944), Michael Daunt, Frank McKenna, Air Commodore Sir Frank Whittle, and W.G. Carter – Gloster's chief designer. *Tony Buttler collection*

Above: DG206/G was the first of its type to fly because its De Havilland H.1 engines became flight ready before the W.2B engines intended for some of the other F.9/40s. As can be seen by comparing photos, the H.1 power unit required portly engine nacelles the drag of which offset the greater power output of the H.1 over the W.2B/23. What, though, was the purpose of the semi-circular device below the aerial mast? Later photos of DG206 show the device to have been removed and a Sky fuselage band added.

Right: DG207/G, the sole Meteor prototype F.2, was powered by two H.1b Goblin engines housed in nacelles similar to those seen on DG206, production of the F.2 was cancelled as Goblin production was required for the DH Vampire. Had production gone ahead, the Mark 2 would have had a slightly larger centre-section, hence a longer wingspan to accommodate the H.1. *Both: Tony Buttler collection*

Meteor F.1

O n 12 January 1944, Meteor F.1 EE210, became the first of its Mark to fly. Originally intended to be the first of 300, it instead became the first of just twenty when the order was cut in April 1943 following doubts about the programme's viability at such an early stage of development.

The F.1 was virtually the same as F.9/40, DG202, the differences of note lay with its two RR Welland 1 engines (i.e. the W.2B/23) which had been upgraded to provide about 1,700 lb of thrust each, an improved canopy for better rearward vision, plus the installation of four 20mm cannon. The F.1's performance can be viewed as adequate, albeit offering little if any speed advantage at medium and higher altitudes over the latest piston-engined designs. However, the F.1 could sustain about 410 mph at sea level which was faster than many piston-engined fighters could achieve when operating at that height – excepting those fitted with engines rated specifically for lower altitudes.

Given that several F.1s were involved in test and development work, it barely seems credible that sufficient could be made available for active service. Yet, by 17 July 1944, the Meteor F.1 had been cleared for service use and later that month 616 Squadron received the type along with most of the men and the machines from the former Tactical Flight, a Meteor unit formed a few months earlier, on 18 March. Additionally, at least four F.1s were periodically operated by 1335 Conversion Unit during the type's short service life which, for most of the survivors, ended in 1946 when they were relegated to ground instructional status.

The last flying F.1 was EE227 which, having served with 616 Squadron, was converted from March 1945 to test a pair of Rolls-Royce RB.50 Trent turboprops in lieu of Wellands. Struck off charge in 1949, EE227 probably made its last flight towards the end of 1948.

Top and above: First flown in April 1944, Meteor F.1 EE211/G offers a reasonable view of the 'short' engine nacelles common to Welland-powered F.9/40s, production F.1s and all but the last fifteen production F.3s. Short nacelles created significant vibration which in turn imposed speed restrictions upon early Meteors. Thus, by March 1945 EE211/G had been experimentally fitted with longer nacelles that ultimately proved successful and were to become standard on the F.4. *Tony Buttler collection*

A familiar image showing Meteor F.1 s and F.3s of 616 Squadron in 1945. The nearest Meteor is F.1 EE219 'YQ-D', while behind is F.3 EE235 'YQ-H', the two Marks employing different style cockpit canopies. EE219 'YQ-D' later became 'YQ-N' and then 5799M in January 1946, while EE235 went on to serve with 1335 CU and the CFE prior to becoming 5781M in 1946. *Via Tony Buttler*

A rear-quarter view of 616 Squadron F.1, EE222/G 'YQ-G', photographed prior to 20 September 1944 – the day it force-landed at Plucksgutter, Kent, after it ran out of fuel. *Via Tony Buttler*

A front-quarter view of F.1, EE223. This airframe never entered RAF service, being retained instead for use by the manufacturer and the A&AEE until, in March 1945, it went to Rolls-Royce to trial the company's RR W.2B/37 engine – better known today as the Derwent 1. EE223 was SOC in 1946. *Tony Buttler collection*

Meteor F.3

The Meteor F.1 was replaced on the production line by the more powerful Meteor F.3 with engines rated at 2,000 lb thrust each, giving the Mark a superior performance over not just its predecessors but its piston-engined contemporaries too. Eventually the F.3 would equip at least seventeen RAF squadrons – albeit not simultaneously it should be noted (see Appendix 1).

The F.3 was powered by the W.2B/37 engine, or the Derwent 1 as it would later be known, although the first fifteen airframes received the earlier Welland because, initially at least, airframe supply outstripped engine supply. EE230 was both the first F.3 and the first of its Mark to fly (in September 1944), while EE245 became the first Derwent-powered F.3. As related earlier, all except the last fifteen F.3s received short 'pop-bottle' engine nacelles – some of which were retrospectively fitted with long nacelles – while some had more powerful 2,400 lb thrust Derwent 4 engines fitted.

Meteor F.3, EE457 'ZD-Q', belonging to 222 Squadron which received F.3s from October 1945. Originally retained by GAC, this Meteor is believed to have been involved in the development of the 'long' engine nacelle, although it wasn't one of the fifteen long-nacelle production F.3s referred to earlier. Long-chord nacelles were first trialled by F.1, EE211, and it was discovered that they almost eliminated buffeting under most conditions – while at sea level (with 2,000 lb thrust engines) EE211's speed increased by almost 60mph. EE457 was written-off on 7 October 1947. *Roger Lindsay collection*

F.3, EE420 'RAA-B', of 500 (County of Kent) Squadron circa 1948. 500 Squadron received its first Meteors in July 1948 and gradually replaced the unit's Mosquito NF.30s over the ensuing months. Finished in High-Speed Silver overall (HSS), EE420, late of 222 Squadron, displays its Reserve Command code 'RAA' ('R' = Reserve) and individual letter 'B' followed by a hyphen which was applied to some of the unit's F.3s but not all. Later recoded 'S7-B', EE420 left the Squadron in October 1951, three months after its first Meteor F.4s arrived. Following a period of storage it became 6968M in May 1952. *Via Roger Lindsay*

F.3, EE305 'RAA-H', of 500 Squadron undergoing maintenance in 1949 complete with screwdriver lodged against the rim of the nose panel. Later coded 'S7-H', EE305 departed the unit in April 1950 and later served with 206 AFS. It was sold for scrap on 22 June 1956. *Newark Air Museum*

Somewhat beyond its prime, 500 Squadron F.3, EE403 'S7-E', is seen in 1952 awaiting the scrap man. The unit code 'S7' (*not* 'SZ') replaced 'RAA' when RAuxAF fighter squadrons were transferred to Fighter Command in November 1949. Most of 500 Squadron's Meteors presented their unit code forward of the roundel on the port side, although a known exception was F.3 EE460 'S7-V', which had 'S7' placed aft of the roundel on both sides of the fuselage. Despite a few exceptions, two-character unit codes were generally discarded during 1951. *Via Roger Lindsay*

As with the F.1, 616 Squadron became the first operational unit to receive the F.3 commencing in the last days of 1944 and into January 1945. Sent to the continent, it was hoped they might engage the Luftwaffe's much-vaunted jets, particularly the Me 262, but, to the mortification of historians and enthusiasts ever since Hitler's jets proved elusive and no such combat occurred.

The Meteor F.3 remained in operational service in diminishing numbers until 1951, when the last two F.3-equipped front line units, Nos.500 and 616 Squadrons Royal Auxiliary Air Force (RAuxAF), received the Meteor F.4 which had begun to equip Regular RAF Fighter Command squadrons from 21 December 1947. Thereafter, some F.3s continued in use as advanced trainers, notably with Nos.205, 206 and 210 Advanced Flying Schools (AFS) into 1954.

616 Squadron Meteor F.3, EE240 'YQ-R' seen while operating over the Continent in 1945. Painted white as a precaution against being misidentified as a Luftwaffe jet. *Tony Buttler collection*

Following wartime service with 616 Squadron as 'YQ-H', F.3 EE236, went on to serve with 1335 CU and then the Empire Central Flying School, coded 'B'. In 1946, Flying Training Command introduced a new three-letter unit code system in which ECFS Meteor F.3s, F.4s and Spitfire 9s were all coded 'FCW' (plus their individual code letters). It seems highly improbable though that EE236 could have received such a code given it became 5786M on 12 January 1946. *Tony Buttler collection*

Disbanded in August 1945, 616 Squadron reformed in 1946 with the Reserve code 'RAW'. Equipped with Mosquito NF.30s in 1947, from January 1949 the Squadron once again operated Meteor F.3s. Although undated, this photo was taken between 31 August 1949, when EE276 'RAW-T' joined the unit, and 8 January 1950, the date on which EE472 'RAW-R' was abandoned following severe icing that caused both engines to quit and neither could be restarted. This image is unusual in showing two of the rare long-nacelle F.3s, EE463 'RAW-N' and 'RAW-R', accompanied by short-nacelle 'RAW-T', beyond; it also shows that only one of the trio sports post-war roundels and fin flash. *Via Roger Lindsay*

Back to 'YQ'. Following the transfer of the Auxiliary squadrons to Fighter Command on 1 November 1949, 616 Squadron reverted to a familiar code. Seen in September 1950, F.3, EE393 displays the code 'YQ-J' as well as a Squadron badge flanked by green and yellow bars on the nose (an adornment marred by muzzle blast) which began to appear at about the same time as the change of code. Meteor F.3s were retained until May/June 1951, F.4s having been received a few weeks earlier in April. *Via Roger Lindsay*

F.3, EE354 'XL-H' from 1335 (Meteor) Conversion Unit. Formed on 8 March 1945 with an intended establishment of 8 Meteor F.1s, 6 Meteor F.3s, Spitfire 18s, Hornets, Oxfords and Martinets, the Unit moved to Molesworth in July 1945, where this photo was taken, and where it was subsequently renamed 226 Operational Conversion Unit on 15 August 1946. EE354 later served with 263, 74 and 63 Squadrons and became 6971M in May 1952. *Via Tony Buttler*

An unidentified F.3 with long nacelles with mesh grills visible. The basic wing shape seen here had been used on all production Meteors so far, and was retained for early production F.4s. It would be used again for the PR.10, NF.11, NF.12, NF.13 and NF.14 too. *Via Tony Buttler*

Meteor F.4

eteor F.3, EE360/G, was selected to become the Meteor F.4 prototype complete with a new powerplant, the Derwent 5, developing 3,500 lb thrust – a significant increase in power over earlier Derwents. As such, EE360 made its first flight on 15 August 1945.

Production F.4s featured a pressurised cockpit and increased internal fuel capacity, the latter enhanced by the provision of a jettisonable 175-gallon ventral fuel tank, plus (later) two 100-gallon wing-mounted drop tanks. To cope with the extra weight, power and speed of the F.4, which was now capable of reaching 585 mph at sea level, it was anticipated that some structural modification would be required and so the Mark's fuselage and wing centre sections were strengthened accordingly. Subsequent experience led to several trials centred upon the F.4's rate of roll which was found to be unacceptable and in need of a remedy. The solution, it was decided, was to 'clip' each wing and reduce the overall span from 43ft to 37ft 2in. Following the completion of one hundred or so 'long-span' F.4s, production turned to the 'clipped-wing' F.4, the top speed of which increased to *circa* 590mph at sea level – although its handling at high altitude, already quite poor, was reduced further.

As stated earlier, Fighter Command began to operate the new Meteor in December 1947 and by late 1950 the Mark was at its peak of operational service. Thereafter the F.4's importance in the UK air defence scene declined, with Fighter Command's last front-line examples having left squadron service by summer 1952.

Several F.4's subsequently received a second lease of life as advanced trainers within OCUs, gunnery schools and various flying training schools, or FTS (in June 1954, surviving advanced flying schools were renumbered and renamed). Other F.4s were used to assist night fighter pilots to convert from piston to jet-power, from Mosquito to Meteor NF.11. (As late as July 1951, Britain still relied solely upon the increasingly inade-

Meteor F.4, 1 Squadron, 1949. Though not positively identified, the aircraft's code 'F' suggests it is VT270 which remained with 1 Squadron until September 1950. Its elongated fuselage stripes weren't unique, as VZ428 'B' (see colour section) was virtually identical save for the latter's post-war markings. Striking to look at, the stripes failed to gain official sanction and were abandoned in 1950. Although the pair didn't display the unit's code 'JX', it was still in use as can be seen on a Meteor further down the line. Individual code letters and fuselage stripes were red. VT270 was converted to a U.15 from April 1955. *Tony Buttler collection*

43 Squadron Meteor F.4, VT276 'SW-N', seen with ventral fuel tank fitted. This image was taken prior to 25 November 1949 – the date when the pilots of VT276 and VT238, while descending through cloud, received an incorrect vector from a ground controller. Both Meteors flew into a hill killing both pilots. *Via Roger Lindsay*

quate and obsolete Mosquito NF.36 for its nocturnal air defences). Finally – absolutely final in fact for most – several F.4s were converted to the role of unmanned flying target and redesignated Meteor U.15.

As s footnote, F.4, VT347, was adapted to become the sole Meteor PR.5 (FR.5 according to some). Fitted with a camera nose and retaining its guns, VT347's first flight in modified form was on 15 June 1949, sadly, it broke up in flight following a high-g manoeuvre and crashed, killing its pilot. (The Meteor F.6 existed as a proposal only.)

Meteor F.4, VZ417 'A', 63 Squadron, seen *circa* mid-1950 when the unit was in the process of relinquishing its code 'UB' in favour of 'fighter bars', in their case using black and yellow chequers. Miniature chequers also flank a Squadron badge on the engine nacelle. Most of the unit's F.4s were replaced by F.8s during January to March 1951, but VZ417 somehow hung on until transferred to 500 Squadron in August. Having later served with 215 AFS and 12 FTS, VZ417 was converted to a U.15 in 1956 and issued to the RN's 728B Squadron. It was shot down at 32,000ft off Malta by a Seaslug missile on 24 August 1960. *Roger Lindsay collection*

Meteor F.4, VT139 'LZ-D', 66 Squadron. Seen in 1949, VT139 pulls out after 'attacking' an Avro Lincoln while a second moves in to make its attack – doubtless the gunner's twin-20s shot both down! The photo is interesting inasmuch that it shows, more clearly than most, where – when fitted – the 175-gallon belly tank would be positioned. *Tony Buttler collection*

A 66 Squadron scene, with an unidentified F.4 in the foreground and VW273 'LZ-E' beyond. It's likely this photo was taken in 1949 as by 1950 most of the unit's Meteors had had their engine intake rims painted blue or red to denote their respective Flights. The panel ahead of the cockpit on the nearest aircraft has become a canvass for the Squadron's rattlesnake motif which 'E' still lacks: the unit motto translated reads 'Beware, I have warned'. *Via Tony Buttler*

F.4, VT231 'MR-N', served with 245 Squadron from August 1948 until mid-July 1950 and is seen in 1950, the year the Squadron badge was transferred from the nose of their Meteors to the engine nacelles – adding miniature bars with blue and yellow chequers as they did so. Readers will quickly notice that the aircraft code 'MR' appears aft of the roundel in some instances and forward of it in others, while VT109 'MR-C' (fourth tailplane along) has a post-war fin flash with a late-war fuselage roundel. VT231 came to grief while serving with 4 FTS on 3 August 1954 when, after an engine failed during a roller landing, it yawed and wiped off its undercarriage. Happily, the pilot survived.
Courtesy of Pavel Turk (via Roger Lindsay)

To include it or not? On balance, yes. It is a crisp image, one of a sequence of now-familiar photos taken of F.4, RA444 'A6-B', of 257 (Burma) Squadron, between February 1948 and May 1949 when this aircraft left the unit. The effigy on the nose is a chinthe (lion-like leogryphs that guard Burmese pagodas) which, by early 1950, had largely been relocated to the engine nacelles flanked by miniature bars with green and yellow chequers. *Via Tony Buttler*

600 Squadron Meteor F.4s seen in 1951 when the unit was obviously at the centre of media attention given the presence of so many photographers with movie cameras atop two of the cars on the right-hand side. From our perspective, however, the most interesting feature concerns the mix of upper wing roundels with three variations on display, while the two nearest the camera display different forms of unit marking below their respective cockpits. Meteor 'X' is VW300 and 'Z' is VW304. (See colour section) *Via Tony Buttler*

Until 31.8.49, the day it disbanded at Driffield, 226 OCU Meteors used codes 'KD' (T.7) and 'XL' (F.3 & F.4). However, 226 OCU reformed next day at Stradishall where F.4, EE517 'HX-L' (the first production Meteor F.4) was photographed in 1950. At this time 226 OCU operated two integral squadrons in which 1 Squadron's Meteors (F.4, T.7, F.8), Spitfires (LF.16e) and Vampires (FB.5) used code 'HX'. 2 Squadron's Meteors and Vampire FB.5s used 'KR', while 'UU' was used by the OCU's FR Flight of Spitfires (F.14, LF.16, PR.19, F.22), Meteor T.7s and, from June 1951, FR.9s – as well as by Station Flight aircraft also. *Roger Lindsay collection*

Seen in 1951, F.4 EE521, from the Central Gunnery School (CGS) is inventively coded 'VG-FJ' when in fact it should read 'FJV-G'. The CGS was allocated consecutive codes FJR to FJX inclusive in 1946 – a reflection of the sheer number of aircraft it was likely to operate. The intention was for the three-letter group to appear together while a fourth – the individual aircraft letter – would be separated by the fuselage roundel. *Roger Lindsay collection*

F.4, EE455 *'Forever Amber'*. Ordered as F.3s, EE454 and EE455 were completed as F.4s and issued to the reformed RAF High Speed Flight after guns and other unnecessaries had been removed and their external surfaces honed to a 'high-speed finish'. On 7 November 1945, over Herne Bay, EE454 *'Britannia'* reached 606 mph and took the world air speed record, while EE455 managed 603 mph. It is often stated that *Forever Amber* was painted overall high-gloss yellow – but this is only partly true as its outer wing sections (and part of its empennage) were polished natural metal. Though the image quality is poor, examination of the engine nacelle area is quite revealing. (See colour section). *Tony Buttler collection*

F.4, EE549, a deception in blue – RAF Innsworth, May 1963. With the Americans attempting to gain the world air speed record, Gloster's prepared two further F.4s, EE549 and EE550, for an attempt to push the speed higher still. Success was achieved by EE549 on 7 September 1946 at 616 mph. EE549 later became the mount of ACM Sir J.M. Robb, was coded 'J-MR' and painted overall light blue – presumably the same blue as per 'his' two Spitfires (LF.16e SL271 'JM-R', and PR.19 PM659 'JM-R'). Grounded in June 1952, EE549 later received the maintenance serial 7008M and was moved to various locations prior to arriving at Innsworth. At some point the airframe was painted blue, possibly in recognition of 'JM-R' or simply because Roundel Blue was in plentiful supply! It may be said too that the style, size and proportions of the roundel and serial number were somewhat unusual! The nose legend refers to 7 September 1946. *Author's collection*.

Despite its quirky (dark) blue days, EE549 survived to be thoroughly and sympathetically restored to its glory days with the RAF High Speed Flight. This photo, taken at Abingdon in September 1980, also reveals the modified cockpit canopy, with small Perspex panels, fitted because larger areas tended to soften and deform as friction increased at high speed. Another point of interest, sometimes overlooked when attempting to interpret colour, Fred has captured a mix of shadow and sunlight, perfectly illustrating how the same colour(s) can appear to be completely different. *Fred Martin collection*

Meteor T.7

Until the arrival of the T.7, pilots new to Meteors were converted to their mount by the simple expedient of having their 'dual' instruction provided by their tutor who, perched on the wing, would lean over the student sat in the cockpit, point to various levers, knobs and dials and utter words of instruction. The student then took off! While this system, the only system, worked for hundreds of Meteor pilots in the early years it could hardly be considered ideal, especially when foreign governments placed orders for the F.4 **and** asked that their novice pilots be taught to fly them.

Thus, a two-seat Meteor would be an obvious asset so, in recognition of the fact, Gloster's adapted a damaged F.4 and rebuilt it as their two-seat demonstrator G-AKPK which first flew on 19 March 1948 powered, as per the F.4, by two Derwent 5s. In fact, official interest already existed and the first production Meteor T.7 made its first flight on 26 October 1948, with initial RAF deliveries probably going to 203 AFS two months later.

In most respects the T.7 was an F.4 albeit with a thirty-inch fuselage extension to accommodate a second seat (in tandem) beneath a single-piece, heavily framed, side-hinging canopy. T.7s were unpressurised, devoid of ejection seats and weaponry and while earlier versions were powered by Derwent 5s later T.7s received the slightly more powerful Derwent 8 offering 3,600 lb thrust.

T.7, WF769 'Q', 66 Squadron, seen at Acklington on 20 September 1958 with a Mosquito T.3 beyond. By this time the unit code was a distant memory, having been replaced by white rectangles thickly outlined in Royal Blue, one of which lies over the yellow trainer band on the rear fuselage. WF769 was SOC less than two months later on 13 November. (See colour section).
Roger Lindsay collection

T.7, WL380, 74 Squadron seen at Bovingdon in 1954. Originally delivered in High-Speed Silver with yellow trainer or 'T-bands' in early 1952, WL380, somewhat unusually for a T.7, was camouflaged in 1954 as seen here. The tiger head on the engine cowling appears at first glance to stand alone, however, a closer look reveals a yellow bar on either side. Perhaps the missing black segments were added next day! WL380 remained in RAF service until transferred to the RAE in 1966. (See colour section). *Via Roger Lindsay*

Seen at Watton in April 1968 is T.7, WL378 'W', of 85 Squadron – *not* to be confused with the Meteor night-fighter/Javelin all-weather unit which disbanded on 31 March 1963. 85 Squadron reformed the following day, largely for use in the fighter intercept training role equipped with Canberras supplemented by Meteor T.7s and F.8s. In addition to the Squadron's red/black Squadron chequer markings, the unit's hexagon can be seen on the fin. WL378 was SOC on 16 August 1972. (See colour section). *Author's collection*

T.7, WF772 'L', 208 Squadron seen at Malta on 14 September 1957. At this time, 208 Squadron was still equipped primarily with the Meteor FR.9 along with one or more T.7s. Almost impossible to see in this image are the Squadron bars on the fuselage which are best appreciated by examining WF772's colour profile. Equally, the apparently black nose marking was in fact blue – denoting the Flight it belonged to. WF772 went on to serve with Malta's Communication & Target Towing Squadron prior to joining 29 Squadron (Javelins) in Cyprus before ending its days on Leuchars' fire dump from May 1968. *Tony Buttler collection*

Indicative of the fact that Meteor T.7s were issued to non-Meteor fighter squadrons is VZ637 'P' of 502 Squadron which was primarily equipped with the Vampire FB.5. Six T.7s were operated by 502 Squadron between April 1951 and March 1957, though not all served concurrently, while VZ637 served the unit from October 1953 until February 1957. Finished in High Speed Silver overall, the two fuselage bars were light blue with a thin red border and contained red lightning flashes with a single bar being repeated on both sides of the aircraft's nose. However, the bar on the port side was surmounted by a small Squadron badge positioned directly above the apex of the central lightning flash. VZ637 was scrapped in October 1962. *Newark Air Museum*

T.7, WA610 'TM-M', of 504 Squadron seen during the period the unit was equipped with the F.4, one of which, VZ401 'TM-K', is partially visible beyond. *Roger Lindsay collection*

T.7, WH208 belonging to Vampire-equipped 612 Squadron. Seen in 1952 with underwing tanks fitted, its code '8W-V' is displayed unconventionally. *Author's collection*

T.7, WA660 was delivered to the RAF in January 1950 and shortly thereafter was allocated to 237 (PR) OCU, by then based at Leuchars, and received the code 'LP-66' as seen here. In 1950, Mosquitoes still remained much in evidence in the post-war RAF and 237 OCU was no exception, as it continued to make good use of its T.3s, PR.34s and B.35s until they were displaced by the Meteor FR.9 and PR.10. Sadly, the Mark and serial number of Mosquito 'LP-95' has thus far defied identification. *Newark Air Museum*

T.7, WH177 'O-H', from the CFS is seen on 15 May 1952. The code ('O' in this case), represented the new system of single letter unit identifiers introduced from 1952 for RAF training aircraft with 'O' being used concurrently by CFS-operated Provosts and Harvards as well – not to mention its use by several AFS and FTS units too. Many other letters were used although M, N, P, plus O, were the most prolific. *Newark Air Museum*

Seen in September 1958 or 1959, T.7, WA725 'Y', belonging to Leuchars Station Flight bears both the saltire of 151 Squadron and chequers of 43 Squadron on its fuselage. Most RAF stations maintained a Station Flight of their own for communications purposes and at Leuchars the fuselage bars tended to reflect the squadrons resident there. On 10 September 1959, WA725 was transferred to 151 Squadron, still coded 'Y', where it remained until August 1961 when it was sent to a MU prior to being scrapped in late 1962. (See colour section). *Tony Buttler collection*

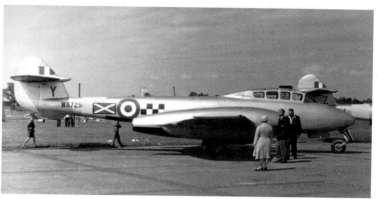

T.7, WH208 '70', 8FTS, Swinderby, 1962. Delivered on 7 February 1952, WH208 served with 611 and 612 Squadrons before moving to the Bomber Command Communication Squadron (BCCS), followed in turn by 5 FTS, 8 FTS, the RAF College of Air Warfare (RAFCAW), and finally 229 OCU. As recorded earlier, this aircraft was damaged while landing at Bovingdon on 23 June 1967 and SOC as a result. 8 FTS reformed at Driffield on 1 June 1954, moved to Swinderby in 1955 and finally disbanded there on 19 March 1964. *Author's collection*

RAE T.7, WA662, Finningley, September 1983. Few British-operated Meteors enjoyed a working life as long as that of WA662, then based at Llanbedr, where it was employed as a hack, a shepherd for Jindivik target drones and for pilot handling and instrument checks – the latter in relation to the few remaining Meteor D.16s presumably. In 1987, WA662 went to Shoeburyness and by January 1988 was to be found upside-down in a test rig at Farnborough. Withdrawn in 1989 the T.7 was despatched to Chalgrove as a source of spares for Martin-Baker Ltd and today resides with the South Yorkshire Air Museum, Doncaster. The striking RAE colour scheme was applied in 1978, while the fuselage disc reads 'International Air Tattoo 1981'. *Fred Martin collection*

Left: Allocated to Javelin-equipped 23 Squadron on 8 November 1956 for communications and target-tug (TT) duties, T.7, WA721, is seen at Coltishall on 14 August 1960. By simply fitting a belly tank with a towing lug, T.7s and other Marks could readily perform basic TT functions using a towed banner on a 200ft cable. Although the lug isn't visible the underside diagonal yellow and black markings, officially specified for target-towing aircraft are, so too is the fuselage T-band. As numbers of T.7s and F.8s became available for TT duties, the latter's designation has sometimes been referred to retrospectively and probably erroneously as the F(TT).8, yet oddly, references to a 'T(TT).7' seem to be virtually unheard of! *Newark Air Museum*

Below: By now serving with Lightning F.1-equipped 74 Squadron following its transfer from 23 Squadron in March 1963 when the latter unit moved to Leuchars, WA721 is seen at Coltishall on 13 August 1963 having at some point received a liberal application of fluorescent day-glo orange, while still retaining areas of Yellow T-bands. By 27 August 1963 the T.7 was in RAF Germany relegated to crash/rescue training duties. (See colour section) *Newark Air Museum*

Above: Added for comparison with WA721, this example has had its T-bands removed and replaced by fluorescent day-glo orange. Photographed at Waddington on 15 September 1962, this T.7 had been operated by 111 Squadron since October 1959. WA671 remained with 'Treble One' until transferred to 74 Squadron in January 1963 and was ultimately SOC at Wildenrath in May 1964. *Newark Air Museum*

Right: A head-on view of T.7, WA669 '02', from the Tactical Weapons Unit (TWU) as seen in June 1978, by which time it numbered amongst the last Meteors in RAF (as opposed to RAE) service. The code '02' appeared on the fin also. (The TWU became 1 TWU when 2 TWU formed on 31 July 1978.) *Fred Martin collection*

Bottom: Transferred in October 1982, WA669 is seen with its CFS motif beneath the cockpit (with an unusual effigy above it), as well as 'The Starship Enterprise' on its fin – which ought to date the photo even if its relevance isn't clear. Subsequently paired with Vampire T.11, XH304, to form the 'Vintage Pair', tragically the duo collided and crashed at Mildenhall on 25 May 1986 killing both Meteor crewmembers. *Fred Martin collection*

T.7, WF791, Finningley 14 September 1963. Delivered in 1951, WF791 initially joined 26 Squadron before being allocated to a succession of training units, of which one was the CFS coded '27'. It later served with 5 Civilian Anti-Aircraft Co-Operation Unit (CAACU) and probably 229 OCU until, at point thereafter, it was allocated a maintenance number (probably not taken up) which, ordinarily, would have meant the end of its flying life. However, WF791 returned to flying status to become part of the RAF's 'Vintage Pair' display team until replaced by WA669. The badge on the nose is that of the CFS. *Author's collection*

T.7, WF791, seen in August 1980 while serving with the CFS whose motif can be seen on the forward fuselage. The victim of a phenomenon known as the 'Phantom Dive', WA791 was destroyed and its pilot killed near Baginton airport, Coventry, during an air display on 30 May 1988. *Fred Martin collection*

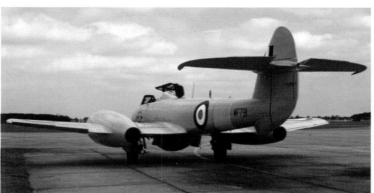

An otherwise bland image revealing the upper surface positioning of this T.7's yellow T-bands. Delivered on 13 May 1952, WL364 was probably photographed prior to its allocation to 202 AFS. Its didn't enjoy a particularly long life as it was written-off on 21 April 1955 at Little Rissington when its undercarriage collapsed – just one of seven Meteors lost during an eight-day period. *Tony Buttler collection*

Included to illustrate a hybrid created by mating an F.8 empennage to an otherwise standard T.7 – resulting in the hybrid T.7½. This image dates from 5 July 1952 when, having returned to GAC for modification, it made the first of ten flights with its new tail which was installed to overcome a tendency to 'snake' at high speed. On 24 July, WA634 was returned to the Martin-Baker Aircraft Company for ejection seat trials and further mods which included an open rear cockpit and a reinforced floor and fuselage to withstand blast damage: it also gained an ejection seat for the pilot, the first T.7 to be so fitted. Now preserved, WA634 resides at the Aerospace Museum, Cosford. *Tony Buttler collection*

Meteor F.8

A formation of 19 Squadron F.8s seen in 1951/52 led by WE863 'A' (unseen on nosewheel door) – its chequered fin obscured both the national marking and individual aircraft letter. The unit's fuselage chequers were Royal Blue and white with two distinct patterns employed – notice how those on the three nearest aircraft differ from the other four. Also, excepting WE863, the tips of their bullet fairings were painted red or blue to denote their respective Flights, while Flight Commanders had the entire fairing painted accordingly – such as WE855 (second from camera).
Via Roger Lindsay

More aerodynamically efficient than the F.4, the F.8 offered certain improvements over the earlier model. The most obvious external differences lay primarily with the adoption of an entirely new tail assembly, the addition of a 30in insert forward of the fuselage centre section (containing ninety-five gallons of additional fuel) and, from mid-1953 onwards, a full clear-view canopy for the pilot. Less obvious was the inclusion of a Martin-Baker 1E ejection seat and the fact that the F.8 was powered by Derwent 8 engines producing 3,500 lb thrust each – the same as the Derwent 5s of the F.4, albeit the latter weighed several hundred pounds less than an F.8.

Two F.4s were used in early F.8 development, RA352 (crashed February 1949) and VT150 which ultimately became the first full F.8 prototype and as such was first flown in October 1948, while the initial production F.8, VZ438, flew in September the following year.

The new day-fighter was destined to be used almost exclusively by Fighter Command for the air defence of the UK until the Mark was released for other duties as more advanced day fighter designs entered RAF service. At least thirty squadrons used the F.8 operationally, the first to receive them being 245 Squadron on 29 June 1950, which, as it transpired, also became the last Fighter Command squadron to relinquish it in June 1957.

The F.8 received several modifications during an operational life lasting barely seven years, but this was sufficiently long enough for its weight to slowly increase and its performance to gradually decline. As many readers will appreciate, later production examples (most of the WK and WL-serialed F.8s for instance) incorporated engine intakes that were 4½ inches greater in diameter than earlier F.8s, thereby increasing thrust to 3,740 lb per engine to partly compensate for incremental weight gains and as such were sometimes referred to as 'deep breathers'.

Once its operational life was over, the F.8, like the T.7, proved versatile and long-lived and was to be used in several subsidiary roles for years to come; in fact, it wasn't until late October 1982 that the last F.8 in *RAF* service, VZ467, was finally demobbed.

Right, top to bottom:
A formation of 41 Squadron F.8s led by the CO's mount. Although the image is undated it is known that WH480 joined the unit on 25 February 1952 and departed in early September 1953. It must have presented an arresting sight with its white/red/white rectangular bars thinly outlined in black upon the fuselage, fin and rudder, and above and below the tailplanes (applied laterally from fin to wingtip). Also evident (just) are: red engine intake lips; the Cross of St. Omer further aft; gloss-black gun ports; and squadron leader's pendant below the cockpit (on both sides). (See colour section) *Via Roger Lindsay*

63 Squadron F.8, WA776 'S', seen at Waterbeach in July 1954, served this unit from November 1950 until September 1955 when it transferred to 610 Squadron. The fuselage chequers were black and yellow and were repeated on the wingtips. The letter 'S' is yellow. Of small interest, other than WA776's old-style canopy, is that the F.8 beyond, probably WA819 'M', still has a short fin flash. The silver aircraft with a hinged canopy is a T.7. WA776 was scrapped in April 1959. *Author's collection*

F.8, WK918 'T', 56 Squadron, May 1955. From February 1954, this unit operated Supermarine Swift F.1s and (later) Swift F.2s but retained a reduced number of F.8s to cover operational duties while the Swifts were evaluated. Found wanting, the RAF terminated Swift flying in March 1955 and ordered them returned to an MU while 56 Squadron continued to fly Meteors until Hunter 5s began arriving two months later. WK918's fuselage chequers were red and white with the rectangles themselves thinly outlined in pale blue. The chequers were repeated on the wingtips, but whether they were outlined in blue isn't clear. Camouflage was reintroduced during 1953/54, a move which in many cases led to F.8 identifying letters being changed from black to yellow as here. *Newark Air Museum*

F.8, WL170, from 64 Squadron seen at Malta in 1961 wearing what appears to be dark grey upper surfaces with a pale blue fuselage band the significance of which is uncertain. 64 Squadron had commenced its transition from the day to night fighter role in late August 1956 when Meteor NF.12s and NF.14s began arriving at Duxford. By August 1958 the unit's transition from Meteor to Javelin FAW.7 had begun – and by the end of September all its Meteors had gone – except two: F.8s WF654 and WL170 which were retained as target tugs. The former left the unit in October 1959 while WL170 was retained until despatched to an MU on 28 February 1961. It was scrapped two years later. *Tony Buttler collection*

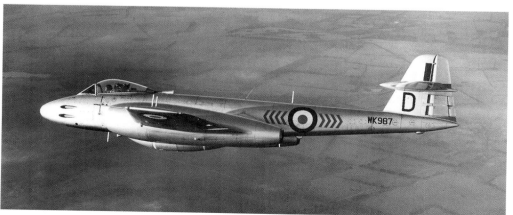

Left: F.8, WK987 'D', 65 Squadron. Seen in late 1953 or early 1954 when it was a member of the unit's four-man display team. Although the unit's red fuselage chevrons are clearly visible, this photo totally fails to 'illuminate' WK987's red-painted ailerons and rudder, not to mention the red segment of its fin flash! *Tony Buttler collection*

66 Squadron's aerobatic team seen in 1951 with F.8 VZ463 'B' leading – with a short fin flash.

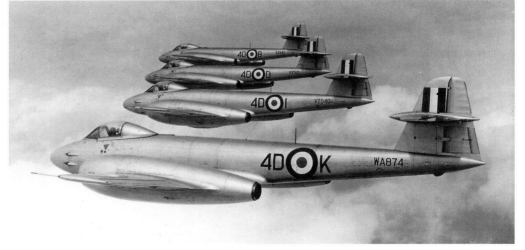

Four 74 Squadron F.8s with WA874, '4D-K', nearest the camera. Just visible above the leading edge of the port wing, on the engine nacelle, is the top of a tiger's head, but whether small unit bars had yet to be added is impossible to determine. WA874 remained with 'The Tigers' from September 1950 until 5 April 1957. (See colour section)

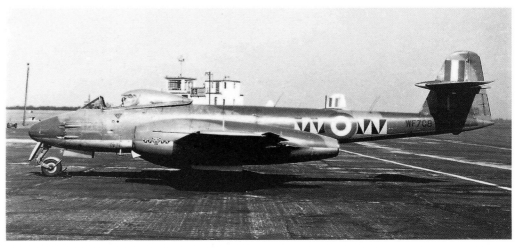

F.8, WF708 'I', 74 Squadron, seen at Bovingdon in 1954 where, unlike T.7 WL380, the black segments of the bars either side of the tiger's head have been applied. 74 Squadron was unusual inasmuch they used the letter 'I' – seen here on the tail, in yellow (repeated on the nosewheel door) whereas most units did not. *All via Roger Lindsay*

85 Squadron F.8, WF654 'Z', seen on approach to Binbrook in June 1969. As noted elsewhere, this unit is not to be confused with the Meteor/Javelin unit that existed until 31 March 1963. 85 Squadron reformed the following day, largely in the fighter intercept training role using Canberras augmented by Meteor T.7s and F.8s. In addition to their red and black chequered markings, the unit's hexagon appears on the fin, while in this instance the intake lips are painted white or light grey. *Tony Buttler collection*

245 Squadron F.8, WA826 'F', complete with Squadron badge on the engine nacelle and yellow and black chequers on the fuselage, is seen undertaking in-flight refuelling (IFR) trials in 1951. This unit was destined to retain the F.8 for longer than any other Fighter Command squadron (29 June 1950 to June 1957) and was the only Meteor squadron to undertake IFR trials. The trials quickly confirmed the value of the concept and were completed by late October 1951, although IFR would not be widely introduced to the RAF until 1960. *Via Tony Buttler*

Seen at Stradishall in July 1955, F.8 WL135, was the mount of 245 Squadron's CO. (See colour section) *Via Roger Lindsay*

245 Squadron F.8, WK947 'W', seen in May 1957 during Exercise *Vigilant*, an air-defence exercise for which the Squadron's Meteors, plus a few Hunters, had their fins painted in white distemper to identify their role as defending fighters. One minor point of interest here is the camouflage demarcation between the upper and lower surfaces which differed from, for instance, 63 Squadron. Following the introduction of camouflage 245 Squadron removed their badge from the engine nacelles. *Newark Air Museum*

Meteor F.8s belonging to 257 and 263 Squadrons seen at Wattisham in 1952. 257 Squadron, on the left, used green and yellow chequers on their elongated bars which were repeated in miniature either side of a forward-facing chinthe on the outer face of each engine nacelle. The chequers were reduced in number in 1953 with the shortened bars outlined in black. One of 257's line still carries the short fin flash. 263 Squadron employed red fuselage bars, each with two dark blue crosses superimposed. The CO's aircraft had a black-painted fin and rudder, while the two Flight Commanders used dark blue and red respectively – one of the latter can be seen at the far end of their line. *Via Roger Lindsay*

Left: Nose detail of F.8, WH454 'A', from 504 Squadron with an officer on the wing showing a young lady his cockpit. A 504 (County of Nottingham) Squadron badge, with their 'Major Oak Tree' motif contained within, is evident on both sides of the nose set upon inverted black shields. *Newark Air Museum*

Below: Meteor F.8, 7354M ex-WE859 'P', seen at Halton in 1958/59. Delivered on 3 May 1951, WE859 went to 600 Squadron as 'P' in August 1955. By 20 June 1956, WE859 had been allocated to 1 School of Technical Training at Halton (SoTT) as 7354M, retaining its 600 Sqn colours on the fuselage. To the left is another ex-600 Sqn F.8 which is believed to be 7294M, previously WF759 'U'. Their identification letters remain as originally applied on 600 Squadron. *Newark Air Museum*

Below right: Meteor F.8, WK988 of 610 Squadron was the CO's aircraft which, unusually, is seen minus its fuselage serial in 1954. The serial was subsequently restored in black. WK988 also featured a red and white striped fin and rudder, a red bullet fairing, Squadron Leader's pennant either side of the cockpit, and the initials 'JAS' on the nosewheel door. Common to all the unit's F.8s were the fuselage bars – black and white with a diagonal serrated division (e.g. see colour illustration of WH384), a Squadron badge on a black disc on the outer faces of the engine nacelles and – just beginning to appear at this time – black-painted wingtips with white leading and trailing tips separated by five white diamonds. *Via Roger Lindsay*

Bottom: A formation of 611 Squadron F.8s with WH365 'D' nearest the camera. All retain their original canopies. Their black fuselage bars contain half-red/half-yellow diamonds displayed alternately – but closer scrutiny reveals WH365's bar pattern to be the opposite of those on the other Meteors. (See colour section). *Newark Air Museum*

Top: Seen in 1953, the CO of 615 Sqn chose WH445 as his mount, hence this F.8's colourful fin, rudder and bullet fairing. Originally delivered to the unit in late October 1951 and coded 'L', it later became 'S' as seen here. *Newark Air Museum*

Centre: In its element – camouflaged 615 Squadron F.8, WF757 'J'. As with WH445, its nosewheel door was blue with a white 'J' superimposed. 'J' is repeated on the fin in dark blue or black. *Newark Air Museum*

Below left: F.8, WL180, belonging to 1574 (Target Facilities) Flight, seen at Singapore, on 12 June 1969 with a TT.20 next in line – probably WD591 which was scrapped in January 1971. Known previously as the Towed Target Flight (Changi), 1574 Flight formed there on 1 May 1964 equipped with T.7s, F.8s and TT.20s to tow targets for Tengah-based Hunters and Lightnings. The black fin and rudder was introduced c 1967. The Flight disbanded on 30 March 1971 and WL180 transferred to Commander Far East Fleet (RN) at Singapore on 26 July 1971. (See colour section). *Author's collection*

Below: F.8, VZ567 'F' serving with 229 OCU on an unrecorded date. Having served in turn with 263, 64, 66 245, 500 and 85 Squadrons (twice) 229 OCU was its last posting. It was scrapped from 15 November 1971. *Author's collection*

F.8, WH291, probably seen during its initial service with 229 OCU. Following service with 257 Squadron and long periods of repair or storage, WH291 was issued in turn to the RAF Flying College (RAFFC), RAFCAW, 85 Squadron from December 1965 until April 1970 and then, following another period of storage, to 229 OCU at Chivenor in October 1970. 229 OCU maintained a handful of Meteors to provide target facilities for the unit's resident Hunters. *Newark Air Museum*

From 2 January 1967 to 2 September 1974 (when it became the TWU), 229 OCU acquired 79 Squadron's number plate as a 'shadow' identity whose red forward-pointing arrows, on white fuselage bars, are seen in this image of WH291. Exactly when it gained its new markings isn't readily apparent, but it was certainly prior to August 1974, the month WH291 returned to 5 MU at Kemble and where it was declared a non-effective airframe (NEA). SOC on 10 February 1976 it was duly preserved. (See colour section) *Fred Martin collection*

Why two near-identical images? Posed as they are, an easy comparison is made between 'deep breather' WH286 and earlier production F.8s such as VZ467. The engine intakes of a 'deep breather' were 4½ inches greater in diameter than the original F.8s, enabling each engine to produce an additional 240 lb of thrust to partly compensate for the type's incremental weight gains acquired in service. WH286 'A' was 'captured' in August 1969 while serving with 229 OCU but by 16 May 1972 was with Flight Refuelling Ltd (FRL) for conversion to a D.16. *Fred Martin collection*

F.8, VZ467 'C', seen while serving with 229 OCU in August 1971. *Fred Martin collection*

F.8, VZ467 '01', from 1 TWU, seen at Finningley in September 1981. Resplendent in 615 Squadron colours, VZ467 never actually served with the latter, although it did serve operationally with 54 and 500 Squadrons. Known as 'Winston' in its later days '01' ('02' was T.7 WA669) became the last flying example of an F.8 in the RAF service. Retired by late October 1982, VZ467 now resides in Australia with a different identity.
Fred Martin collection

WL181 leads WH301 and WL190 in this nicely composed photograph in which, other than the fact all are F.8s, none are identical in terms of colours and markings. Based at Manby, the home of the RAFFC (or RAFCAW as the former was restyled on 1 July 1962), these three Meteors formed part of (or all of ?) the College's aerobatic team. The photograph itself is marked simply 'RAFFC' without any date, however, it certainly pre-dates 9 August 1963, the date when WL190 was SOC. (See colour section: WL181.)
Newark Air Museum

Belonging to the RAFCAW, F.8, WK968 originally coded 'A', but subsequently changed to 'C', sits nearby an unidentified T.7 on an undisclosed date. The RAFCAW eventually disbanded on 1 April 1974, by which time Meteors had been dispensed with. WK968 was declared NEA on 10 July 1969, following which it became a gate guard at Odiham in 1970 serialed 8053M and was scrapped from January 1991.
Newark Air Museum

Above: F.8, VZ508 was delivered to the RAF's Temperature and Humidity Flight (THum Flight) at Woodvale *circa* October 1957 where it, at least one other F.8, and possibly a T.7 were acquired to supplement Mosquito TT.35s. The latter were received from 1956 to replace the RAF's last operational Spitfires – three PR.19s – whose impending retirement was set for June 1957. Absorbed by 5 Civilian Anti-Aircraft Co-operation Unit (CAACU) on 1 January 1958 at Woodvale, THum Flight was disbanded altogether on 1 May 1959, by which point their Meteors had flown relatively few weather-related sorties. VZ508 passed to 5 CAACU that month and is seen here in May 1966 with Exeter-based 3/4 CAACU Vampire T.11, XH329, beyond. By 1968, possibly earlier, VZ508 had been returned to a green & grey upper surface camouflage scheme. *Fred Martin collection*

Left: F.8, VZ508 seen on 17 May 1971 while still in the hands of 5 CAACU which was just four months away from disbandment. VZ508 was converted to a D.16 from the following February. *Newark Air Museum*

Below: Seen in May 1953, WK927 belonged to 12 Group Communications Flight and was used by AVM Sir Richard Atcherley, hence its code 'R-A', and was unusual in insomuch that it was painted Dark Green overall. By 1955 the F.8 had received a full clear-view canopy, the letters 'R-A' had been removed, and a glossier Dark Green replaced the duller shade previously used. (See colour section) *Author's collection*

Right: F.8, WH293 'Y' was delivered to Leuchars-based 43 Squadron, a Hunter unit, on 8 May 1956 for TT duties and remained with the unit until 14 October 1959. According to records WH293 was then sent to 33 MU where it lingered until scrapped in late 1963. The record is incomplete of course given that WH293 was transferred to the Leuchars Station Flight, possibly to replace T.7, WA725 q.v. (also coded 'Y'), following the latter's transfer to 151 Squadron on 10 September 1959. Photographed on an unspecified date, WH293 wears 151 Squadron's saltires and 43 Squadron's chequers on its fuselage. Certainly, WH293 did end up at 33 MU as photos exist of it there wearing precisely the same bars and TT stripes. *Newark Air Museum*

Photographic Reconnaissance

The Meteor FR.9 (Fighter Reconnaissance) differed from the F.8 insomuch that the former was fitted with a pressurised and heated camera nose to thus extend the overall length of the FR.9's fuselage by 9ins. Three glass panels were incorporated to allow for oblique or straight-ahead photography. Most FR.9s carried a single F.24 camera within the nose, however, from late 1953, a few FR.9s were modified to carry Vinten F.95 cameras which, while offering greater clarity at high speed and low altitude, were smaller and lighter than the F.24, and held film for far more exposures than the hundred available to the F.24.

Production FR.9s were delivered from March 1950 and were used operationally by 2 and 79 Squadrons in West Germany and 208 Squadron in the Middle East, although 8 Squadron, a Venom unit operating in Aden, acquired four FR.9s in early 1958 from 208 Squadron as the latter became due to receive Hunters. In June 1958, the FR function was transferred to the Khormaksar Station Flight for three months until the Aden Peninsular FR Flight was formed to operate the remaining FR.9s. Withdrawn by about March 1960, they were the last of their breed in the RAF and almost the last single-seat Meteors in *operational* RAF service – a distinction that finally went to the PR.10s of 81 Squadron in the Far East which operated the type into July 1961.

The Meteor PR.10 (Photo Reconnaissance) was destined for the high-altitude strategic reconnaissance role and was something of a hybrid in its way combining as it did the long-

FR.9, VZ603 'B-A', from 2 Squadron, was the CO's aircraft as identified by the letter 'A' and emphasised by the Squadron Leader's pennant on the nose. 'B' was the 2 Tactical Air Force (2TAF) unit identifier for this squadron which remained in use until replaced by fuselage bars in early 1954. But before that, in 1952, most of the unit's FR.9s were camouflaged in the newly-adopted 2TAF scheme consisting of Dark Green and Dark Sea Grey with PRU Blue under surfaces, while a few received an alternative scheme consisting of Light Slate Grey and Medium Sea Grey upper surfaces and PRU Blue under surfaces with a high fuselage demarcation line. Those painted in the latter scheme each had blue-tipped bullet fairings. (See colour illustrations of FR.9 WX965) *Newark Air Museum*

Unidentified FR.9. *Newark Air Museum*

span wings of the F.3, an F.4's fin and rudder, the centre fuselage of the F.8 and an FR.9's nose. No guns were fitted, but two F.52 cameras in the rear fuselage supplemented the F.24 in the nose. All cameras were heated and pressurised while the ventral cameras were provided with jettisonable metal covers over the ports to protect them when taxying and taking off. Deliveries to the RAF commenced in December 1950, the type being used primarily by 13, 81 and 541 Squadrons with some gravitating in small quantities to other reconnaissance units too. (See Appendix 3: Meteor Reconnaissance Squadrons)

Top left: FR.9 nose and camera ports circa 1953. 'R' was a 208 Squadron aircraft – probably VZ578. The unit's custom was to apply the appropriate Flight colour to each nose cone (later extended further aft), usually either red or blue, although yellow might also have been used at this time. By the time camouflage had been introduced yellow noses were certainly evident. (See colour section – FR.9 WL263) *Newark Air Museum*

Top right: FR.9, WB116 'G' from 2 Squadron in 1954. Following the introduction of camouflage, the unit applied a red Wake Knot on a black disc to the outside of each engine nacelle from early 1953, while black fuselage bars containing white triangles had, by the time this photo was taken, replaced the earlier two-letter code system. WB116's sports a red-tipped bullet fairing denoting 'A' Flight. *Newark Air Museum*

Above: A view of PR.10, VZ620. *Author's collection*

Left: An undated close-up of Laarbruch-based 541 Squadron PR.10, 'D'. One source suggests that this is VW376, however, www. images exist showing the latter to be 'A-C' ('A' being the Squadron code until early 1954). So, did VW376's individual code letter change at some point? The lettering on the white strip reads 'FG OFF M J SOMERVELL'. While 'D' wears the 2TAF colour scheme of Dark Green and Dark Sea Grey with PRU Blue under surfaces, some of this unit's PR.10s wore Medium Sea Grey upper surfaces and PRU Blue under surfaces with a high fuselage demarcation line. (See colour illustration of 13 Squadron PR.10 WB177 'C' for an example of this scheme). *Newark Air Museum*

Bottom: The first production PR.10, VS968 'W', taxies at Wildenrath in August 1955. Evident here is the Squadron badge, equally evident is the band around its rear fuselage. Was it a tactical marking, and what colour was it? I'm afraid we were unable to provide an answer to either question. *Via Roger Lindsay*

The Night Fighters NF.11/13 & 12/14

As used as we are today to Britain's much-depleted and underfunded armed forces, it seems scarcely believable that in early 1950, not five years since World War II had ended, Britain's night fighter defences relied solely upon a handful of Mosquito NF.36s. With a combined paper complement of forty-eight aircraft and an average operational availability of perhaps thirty, spread amongst six squadrons at just two UK locations, it meant that much of Britain's nocturnal skies lay completely unprotected despite an ever-increasing threat from the Soviet Union. To make matters worse, the RAF in Germany had no night fighters allocated to it at all and

NF.11, WD597, illustrates in plan a new shape in the skies. In fact the wing form was essentially that of the Meteor F.3 and early F.4s albeit they now housed the cannon displaced by the redesigned nose (the inner pair of guns are unshrouded). Many pilots preferred the concentrated fire of Meteor day fighters over the somewhat dispersed fire of the night fighters. *Tony Buttler collection*

…and in profile.
Author's collection

Looking a little worse for wear, NF.11, WD776 'D' only served with 5 Squadron from January to September 1959, and so it's likely this image was taken at 33 MU after a couple of years of open storage. Nevertheless, it does illustrate the early camouflage scheme of Dark Green and Medium Sea Grey, with a black aircraft letter on the fin – which was usual for 5 Squadron Meteors in this scheme. It also shows the Squadron's solid red fuselage bars which, unusually, are 'squared-off' – that is they don't conform to the arc of the fuselage roundel. WD776 was scrapped on 31 January 1962. *Roger Lindsay collection*

NF.11, WD663 'C', from 5 Squadron seen during a visit to Hullavington having flown in from its home base, Laarbruch, in September 1959. WD663 wears the later camouflage scheme consisting of Dark Green and Dark Sea Grey with Light Aircraft Grey under surfaces, white serial and white aircraft letter. In the event this unit became the last operational RAF squadron to fly the NF.11. *Roger Lindsay collection*

NF.11, WD641 possibly coded 'F', belonging to Geilenkirchen-based 11 Squadron which operated this Meteor from January 1959 to February 1960: it is painted Dark Green and Dark Sea Grey with Light Aircraft Grey under surfaces and has a red bullet fairing on the fin. Later converted to a TT.20, WD641 went on to serve with 1574 Flight at Singapore until scrapped at Seletar in January 1971. *Via Roger Lindsay*

No, they are **not** '30 Squadron' machines, these NF.11s are from 29 Squadron which became the first to operate Meteor night fighters on 20 August 1951. (But not the RAF's first jet night fighter squadron, that distinction fell to 25 Squadron when it received Vampire NF.10s in July 1951.) Based at Tangmere, WD641 'C' and WD725 'F' are seen in formation in June 1953 displaying their white fuselage bars, outlined in red, with three red 'X's superimposed. The white element was introduced in 1952, prior to which, other than for the 'X's, the bars were hollow. Serials and aircraft codes were black while the tip of the bullet fairing was red. *Via Tony Buttler*

so occasional detachments had to be sent from Britain to provide a fig-leaf defence. As outmoded as Britain's day fighter squadrons were the night fighter situation was much worse, especially when it became evident in early 1949 that the Soviet's contemporary far-ranging Tu-4 'Bull' strategic bomber (née B-29 Superfortress) could fly high enough and fast enough to present a difficult challenge to any Mosquito.

Both de Havilland and Glosters responded to a 1947 Air Ministry requirement to procure jet-powered night fighters, but because of the latter's ongoing commitment towards the development and production of day fighters, PR aircraft and, ultimately, their Javelin all-weather fighter, Glosters were unable to take on the production of what might be considered an 'interim' night fighter. Consequently, Meteor night fighter production would be undertaken by Armstrong Whitworth.

A mock-up of the new Meteor night fighter, the NF.11, was complete by late 1948, while T.7, VW113, became the aerodynamic test-bed for the Mark. Long-span wings, as used on the F.3, were fitted, not just to accommodate the four 20mm cannon displaced from the nose by AI (Air Intercept) radar, but also to balance the new, much longer nose, radar and associated apparatus. VW113 first flew in its new guise on 28 January 1949 and received an F.8-type tail two months later.

The prototype NF.11, WA546, first flew on 31 May 1950 while the first production machine, WD585, made its first flight on 19 October 1950. The NF.11 entered service in August 1951 fitted with AI.10 (US centimetric SCR720) radar dating back to the middle of WWII but was practically obsolete by 1951.

The NF.13 entered service in March 1953 and was basically a tropicalised NF.11 featuring a cold air unit for the cockpit and crew, plus a radio compass which combined to increase its weight by 450 lb over the NF.11. Most NF.13s went to the Middle East to serve with 39 and 219 Squadrons.

The NF.12 incorporated an improved radar – a modified version of the US-designed AN/APS-57 (AI.21 in British service) – which necessitated a further extension to the nose. The new Mark was powered by a pair of Derwent 9s rated at 3,800 lb thrust per unit in lieu of the up-rated Derwent 8s (3,700 lb) fitted to the NF.11 and NF.13. The obvious external difference between the NF.12 and the two earlier Marks concerned the fin. Small fillets were added to its leading edge, both above and below the bullet fairing, to increase fin area and so compensate for the NF.12's increased length and to overcome a tendency for fin stalling at altitude. The first NF.12s entered squadron service on 5 March 1954.

The NF.14 was in most respects the same as the NF.12, the most obvious change being the substitution of the earlier side-hinged heavily framed canopy of the three preceding Marks with a clear-vision sliding canopy.

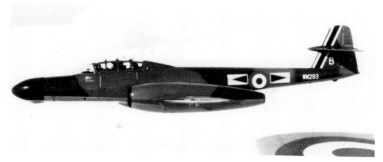

NF.11, WM293 'B' from 68 Squadron which reformed at Wahn, Germany, on 1 January 1952 before moving to Laarbruch in July 1957. This is a post-July 1958 image, the month WM293 joined the unit, but precedes 21 January 1959 – the day 68 disbanded to become 5 Squadron. Each fuselage bar was pale blue (outlined in black) with a dark blue triangle superimposed, the latter outlined in yellow. The pennant under the cockpit marks this as the CO's aircraft, endorsed by the stripe on the fin which in sequence was coloured yellow, pale blue, dark blue, pale blue, yellow. The engine intake lips were black. Later converted to a TT.20 and used by 3/4 CAACU, WM293 was sold to France on 11 December 1974 and broken up for spares. *Via Roger Lindsay*

A formation of 85 Squadron NF.11s, a unit frequently referred to in this book so far. This image, however, was taken at a time when the Squadron was still operational in the night fighter role, a role it would continue to fulfil using Meteors and Javelins until 1963. *Via Roger Lindsay*

87 and 68 Squadrons reformed at Wahn, on 1 January 1952 – two of the four squadrons allocated to 2TAF to provide a measure of nocturnal defence that the RAF in Germany had (almost) completely lacked since the end of WWII. 87 Squadron NF.11, WD673 'F', seen in 1956/57, displays its white fuselage bars (thinly outlined in black) with a black horizontal bar running through the centre entwined by a green 'rope' – in fact it represents a serpent's coil. The photo is perhaps useful in that it gives an indication of the colour of a neoprene-treated radome. *Tony Buttler collection*

Probably taken in 1957, 96 Squadron NF.11, WD794 'H', is seen while taking off at Ahlhorn, Germany where the unit had reformed on 17 November 1952 with 256 Squadron. The fuselage bars were dark blue with yellow 'lightning' flashes, while just aft of the neoprene-coated radome the Squadron badge can just be seen. *Via Roger Lindsay*

141 Squadron NF.11, WD644 'W' was withdrawn from service on 16 November 1954. Originally the unit's NF.11 intake lips were painted black, outlined in white, which were later amended to black, white, black as seen here. Following withdrawal, WD644 appears to have spent several years languishing at both 8 and 20 MU until finally being scrapped on 5 June 1958. (See colour section) *Tony Buttler collection*

NF.11, WM223 'U', seen while serving with Leuchars-based 151 Squadron and displaying the unit's fuselage bars consisting of a St. Andrew's cross on a blue background outlined in black. Squadron bullet fairings were painted red or blue according to which Flight a fighter belonged – WM223's appears to be blue, as does its aircraft letter. Initially aircraft letters were applied in black but this later changed to either red or blue according to Flight allocation. The Squadron badge was applied to the left side of the nose on most of their NF.11s for a time but was later removed. *Via Roger Lindsay*

Another view of WM223 'U' from 151 Squadron. This is a later image as evidenced by the black intake lip – a relatively late addition to 151's fleet. WM223 served with the unit from early December 1953 to February 1956 and was then stored. Following conversion to TT.20 standard it was allocated to 3/4 CAACU until October 1970 when it went into storage and where it remained until SOC in February 1975. *Via Roger Lindsay*

WD585, the first production NF.11 gravitated to 256 Squadron in January 1955. Coded 'B' it was retained until 1 October 1957 then stored at 20 MU prior to being acquired by the RN. Flown to Lossiemouth, it was again stored pending conversion to TT.20 standard which was complete by January 1960. Cocooned in December 1962, WD585 was scrapped in late 1966. In this image WD585 displays its distinctive fuselage bar colours comprising a pale blue segment and a lower dark blue lower segment divided by a white wavy line: less distinct is the red fin bullet. *Via Roger Lindsay*

Many, perhaps most NF.14s, received a R3697 passive warning radar in the extreme tail in lieu of the original tail cone – when fitted it reduced the overall fuselage length by 3½ inches.

NF.14 deliveries commenced in April 1954 and the type remained operational until finally withdrawn from use by 60 Squadron at Singapore in August 1961, by which time its potential opposition, the Soviet Union's much faster Tu-16 'Badger' had been in service for about six years. On 17 August 1961, WS787 'G' made the last ever operational flight of a Meteor fighter in the RAF, having outlived the only other operational RAF Meteor unit (81 Squadron with PR.10s) by about a month.

NF.11, WM234 'U', seen while serving with Linton-on-Ouse based 264 Squadron sometime between January and August 1954 when it departed the unit. Although 'fuzzy' the fuselage bars are reasonably clear, each of which has two broad black bands and one thin one separated by two yellow ones. The aircraft letter on the fin would have been either red or blue depending on which Flight it belonged to. *Via Roger Lindsay*

NF.11, WD752, 'G', from Leeming-based 228 OCU. This was the principal night fighter training unit and operated NF.11s from 23 January 1952 until December 1958, supplemented by the NF.12 and NF.14 from 1954, with a few of the latter remaining on strength until July 1961, just prior to the unit disbanding on 15 September 1961. WD752's aircraft letter 'G' on the fin was green, while that on the nosewheel door was white superimposed on a green hexagon. It later went to 5 Squadron and was scrapped in January 1962. *Via Roger Lindsay*

NF.13, WM311 'X', was withdrawn from use by 39 Squadron on 7 July 1958 and sent to 20MU where it was scrapped on 29 December that year. The Squadron's fuselage bars were black containing a pair of yellow triangles within each. During 'Suez', several of the unit's NF.13s had temporary black and yellow stripes applied which, in at least one instance, obscured one of the triangles in the rearmost segment of the fuselage bars. *Roger Lindsay collection*

Reportedly, one or two 39 Squadron NF.13s were repainted with Dark Green and Dark Sea Grey upper surfaces and it looks as though WM363 'X' might have been one of them (as was WM315), whilst still retaining the high demarcation. The black aircraft letter on the fin (possibly outlined in yellow) is repeated, albeit in a light colour, on the nosewheel door. WM363 was sent to 20 MU in July 1958 and scrapped the following year. *Author's collection*

219 Squadron was the other RAF squadron to re-equip with the NF.13, albeit only for a short time. Here WM312 (uncoded) displays the unit's black fuselage bars with a red chevron superimposed. Clearly visible forward of the ventral fuel tank are the two intakes associated with the cockpit cooling system. Delivered to 219 in April 1953, WM312 served until September 1954 when it was flown to the UK and stored. Purchased by the manufacturer in May 1956, WM312 was subsequently refurbished and sold to Israel as 4X-FNC. *Via Roger Lindsay*

Uncoded NF.13, WM321 from 219 Squadron. WM321 made an emergency landing on 30 April 1954 after suffering an in-flight fire and was later written-off. Purely as general observation, for which exceptions must surely exist – and for which no explanations have been encountered – most 219 Squadron Meteors appear to have had 'half-black' radomes whereas those on 39 Squadron machines seemed to be almost totally black. (See colour section) *Newark Air Museum*

Having become the world's first jet night fighter squadron when it received the Vampire NF.10 in July 1951, 25 Squadron later re-equipped with Meteor NF.12s from 5 March and NF.14s from 1 April 1954 – the two being operated concurrently given that, operationally speaking, they were near-identical Marks. The unit disbanded on 1 July 1958, but was resurrected immediately when 153 Squadron was renumbered. Fuselage bars were silver with black horizontal borders; aircraft fin letters were white on a Flight-coloured disc (red or dark blue accordingly) with a Flight-coloured bullet fairing tip to match. Photographed on 30 April 1954, NF.12, WS697 'N', served with the unit until 26 June 1958. (See colour section) *Via Tony Buttler*

A mixed formation of 46 Squadron NF.12s and NF.14s illustrating the colour schemes predominantly applied to the two Marks – the upper surfaces of the NF.14s are darker in appearance. (See camouflage and markings section). 46 Squadron bars were white with a single arrow head, outlined in red, bisecting the fuselage roundel. *Via Roger Lindsay*

NF.14, WS755 'C' from 60 Squadron, seen in the UK during June or July 1959, was one of fourteen (or sixteen) refurbished NF.14s (note cooling intakes below cockpit *à la* NF13) prepared for service in Singapore to provide a night fighting capability prior to the arrival of Javelins (commencing 13 July 1961). WS755 arrived there in November 1959 and remained with the Squadron until disposed of on 4 July 1961. The fuselage bars of the Singapore-based Squadron – black, outlined in white, each with a white lightning flash – were stylistically different from those employed by the 'old' UK-based NF.12/NF.14-equipped 60 Squadron when training for their forthcoming Far Eastern deployment. *Fred Martin collection*

Finished in Dark Green/Dark Sea Grey and Light Aircraft Grey is NF.12, WS617 'A', from 64 Squadron. Seen on 14 September 1957, this aircraft was operated by the unit from 6 May 1957 to October 1958 when it was despatched to 60 MU. The fuselage markings consisted of a red and dark blue trellis either side of the roundel while the aircraft letter was yellow. The white fin marking was white (thinly outlined in dark blue) and contained a dark blue scarab beetle. Engine intake lips were black. *Newark Air Museum*

Finished in overall Medium Sea Grey with Dark Green disruptive upper surfaces is NF.12, WS611 'N', from 72 Squadron. WS611 was operated by this unit from February 1956 until 11 July 1958, the day it was written off after its undercarriage was damaged when taking off at Church Fenton. *Newark Air Museum*

NF.12, incorrectly serialed 7065M (instead of 7605M), ex-WS692 'C' is seen in June 1975 having formerly served with 72 Squadron until despatched to Henlow in 1959. The following sixteen years had taken its toll of course, but 72 Squadron's red-bordered solid blue fuselage bars are still evident, as indeed is part of the upper camouflage pattern courtesy of an unfortunate incident with the starboard undercarriage. (The serial 7065M properly belonged to Vampire F.1, TG312, incidentally.) Today WS692 appears in infinitely better condition, in a hangar, at Newark Air Museum wearing much the same markings. *Newark Air Museum*

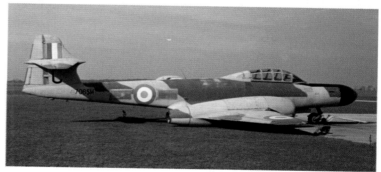

Having previously been equipped with the NF.11, 85 Squadron was re-equipped with NF.12s and NF.14s in 1954, to which the unit's colourful fuselage markings (previously described) were of course applied, as was their distinctive black/white hexagon on the fin. This photo, taken on 24 May 1954, shows NF.14s WS741, WS740 (leading) and WS723. *Tony Buttler collection*

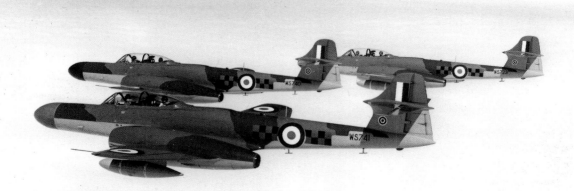

Uncoded NF.14, WS723, seen between April 1954 and February 1955. Until 1956 the tip of 85 Squadron's bullet fairings were painted in the Flight colour (red or blue) but by mid-1956 the policy appears to have changed to black tips only with black intake lips.
Tony Buttler collection

NF.14 WS744 was operated by 85 Squadron until 26 February 1957 when it was converted to an NF(T).14. WS744 was later operated by 2 ANS and 1 ANS until finally grounded in June 1967.
Tony Buttler collection

NF.14, WS755 'B', from 152 Squadron seen in 1956. It was later refurbished and allocated to 60 Squadron for service at Singapore. Could the brownish coloured object at the extreme tip of the fuselage be an R3697 passive warning radar perhaps? *Tony Buttler collection*

NF.12, WS604 'U', seen here in August 1957, was one of just five NF.12s allocated to 264 Squadron to supplement its NF.14s and thus maintain unit strength at sixteen aircraft. The fuselage bars remained the same as when equipped with NF.11s. The aircraft letter on the fin was usually applied in the appropriate Flight colour (either red or blue). WS604 subsequently served with 33 Squadron, the only NF.12 to do so. *Via Roger Lindsay*

NF.14, WS810 'B', also from 264 Squadron, is seen between October 1954 and March 1957 and, although difficult to see, the aircraft letter 'B' on the fin is coloured red to denote A Flight. The unit was renumbered 33 Squadron in late September 1957 and WS810 'V' (its aircraft letter had altered in March 1957) became one of the unit's fifteen NF.14s (with NF.12, WS604, as described above). Later refurbished, WS810 went to 60 Squadron at Singapore. *Newark Air Museum*

The NF(T).14

By the later 1950s, increasing numbers of Meteor NF.14s had become surplus to requirements following the steady introduction of the Javelin to RAF service from February 1956. Consequently at least fourteen airframes were converted for use as trainers to provide further training for navigators destined for fast jet operations for which, with radar removed and UHF radios installed, modified NF.14s became NF(T).14s.

Initially allocated to 2 Air Navigation School (ANS) at Thorney Island, all NF(T).14s were transferred to 1 ANS at Stradishall in early 1962 where they continued in use until February 1966 when they were replaced by Dominies. Both units also made use of T.7s for pilot conversion.

This immaculate NF(T).14, WS797 'O', from Stradishall-based 1 ANS, was seen at Benson in September 1964. Painted High Speed Silver overall, day-glo strips were liberally applied.
Newark Air Museum

Three NF(T).14s from 1 ANS in formation c 1963. WS744 leads WS726 (on the left) and WS774. At first glance the day-glo on all three appears identical – but variations are there.
Newark Air Museum

NF(T).14 WS842 'B' from 2 ANS seen in September 1959. 2 ANS aircraft often had a red diamond applied to their fuselage with the roundel superimposed, but as can be seen this had yet to be applied. Following transfer to 1 ANS, WS842 was stripped of its camouflage and painted High Speed Silver. (See camouflage and markings section).
Newark Air Museum

2 ANS, NF(T).14, WS774 'D', seen with the School's red diamond on its fuselage. Valettas and a Canberra appear in the background. WS774 was later preserved and now resides in Malta.
Tony Buttler collection

Targets, Tugs and RN Meteors

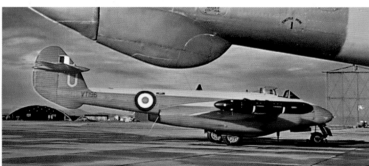

U.15 & D.16

The Meteor U.15 and D.16 (initially referred to as the U.16) were unmanned target drones, converted from surplus Meteor F.4s and F.8s respectively, for use in the development of ground and air-launched guided missiles for which expendable targets were required. They replaced piston-engined Fairey Firefly U.8s and U.9s which were no longer fast enough to adequately represent the sort of targets guided missiles were being designed to hit.

The prototype U.15, RA421, made its first flight as such on 11 March 1955. Approximately ninety further F.4s were converted, followed in turn by about 115 F.8s once U.15 stocks began to dwindle – of which fifteen U.15s and four D.16s were allocated to the Royal Navy. In Britain, Llanbedr was the location where most of the work concerned with target drones was centred.

TT.20

Converted from redundant NF.11s, the Meteor TT.20 was procured by the Royal Navy as a high-speed target tug to replace their ageing Short Sturgeon and Firefly tugs. From the beginning of 1958, twenty-five surplus RAF Meteor NF11s were converted by Armstrong Whitworth into high speed target

Meteor U.15, RA420, seen at Llanbedr on an undisclosed date, had an unusual nose profile the significance of which is unknown to the authors: was it a camera installation and was it unique? RA420's colour scheme – overall Signal Red with Yellow upper surfaces – became synonymous with the drones, although initially the first few were painted High Speed Silver overall but could be distinguished from standard F.4s by their small black dorsal domes, as well as their wingtip-mounted cameras if carried. RA420 was finally written off, presumably intentionally, on 19 February 1962. *Author's collection*

U.15, VT196 'U'. VT196 made the last flight of any U.15 – on 9 February 1963. *Author's collection*

Meteor D.16, WH453 'L' as seen in August 1985. WH453 was withdrawn from flying duties for use as a static test frame in October 1990. *Fred Martin collection*

Meteor D.16, WK800 'Z' as seen in August 1979. Interestingly this aircraft was transferred to the RAAF in February 1953 and was later converted to an Australian U.21A drone. It returned to the UK in July 1971 and took up its original serial number once again. Subsequently modified to a D.16, WK800 lasted until 2004 when it was finally retired and preserved. *Fred Martin collection*

tugs for the RN equipped with a wind-driven ML Aviation Type G winch mounted above the starboard wing between the fuselage and the engine nacelle. This controlled a cable approximately 6,000ft long that was capable of towing Rushton sleeve and banner targets for air-to-air and surface-to-air target practice, and considered to be superior to the TT-lugs fitted to T.7/F.8 ventral fuel tanks. The TT.20 had a crew of two, with the second crewman operating the winch and the cable cutter in the event of an emergency. As the winch, cable and targets were roughly the same weight as the night fighter's armament and radar equipment (all of which were

This is probably WD767, the prototype TT.20. This image is included primarily because it provides a reasonable view of a wind-driven ML Aviation Type G winch. *Tony Buttler collection*

TT.20, WD630 'Q', from Exeter-based 3/4 CAACU, seen in July 1964. WD630 was long-lived and wasn't scrapped until 24 March 1975 after having spent a few years in storage following the CAACU's closure on the last day of 1971. *Author's collection*

TT.20, WD647 'S' from 3/4 CAACU on an unknown date. On 7 August 1970, WD647 was allocated to Flight Refuelling Ltd for use at the Weapons Research Establishment at Woomera. Following its withdrawal from service it went to the Queensland Air Museum in July 1975. Author's collection

TT.20, WD646 'R', from Woodvale-based 5 CAACU, seen in July 1964 while fitted with what appears to be a replacement rudder. Following withdrawal from WD646 was subsequently preserved. *Author's collection*

TT.20, WM270 'Y', previously of 3/4 CAACU is seen while stored and awaiting its fate in September 1974. Several TT.20s were retained in storage partly because France still operated NF.11s and NF.14s at the C.E.V (*Centre d'Essais en Vol – Flight Test Centre*) at Brétigny-sur-Orge where they were used as testbeds and chase planes in a wide variety of experiments. Consequently, as late as December 1974 a half-dozen stored TT.20s (minus TT apparatus) were flown to France (using the civil mark F-ZABD) to be broken up for spares. WM290, however, was stored at 5 MU in October 1970, declared NEA on 30 April 1973, and finally SOC for scrap in September 1975. *Fred Martin collection*

Royal Navy TT.20, WD780 as seen in June 1969, its undersides painted black and Saturn Yellow as opposed to the RAF's preference for Golden Yellow. Despatched to 5 MU in March 1971, WD780 was sold to France as a source of spares for the CEV in November 1974.
Fred Martin collection

Royal Navy TT.20, WM292 '841' seen while operating with the Fleet Requirements Unit (FRU), Hurn, between September 1966 and May 1969. WM292 was allocated to the FAA Museum on 4 June 1969.
Newark Air Museum

TT.20s stored at 5 MU, Kemble, in September 1974. This image provides a comparison between Golden Yellow and the paler Saturn Yellow applied to many of the RN's TT.20s, which was sometimes referred to as 'lime-green' in the sixties as few were as yet aware of its actual name! Identified here is WD592 'HF' and WD630 'Q' (RN and RAF respectively), while the nose of the nearest TT.20 belonged to WM270 'Y'.
Fred Martin collection

removed), the TT.20 had roughly the same performance as the NF.11.

The TT.20 entered FAA service in 1958, with 728 NAS at Hal Far, Malta, where it was used to tow gunnery targets for ship and shore batteries, but most of the aircraft served with the Aircraft Handling Units (AHUs) or Fleet Requirements Units (FRUs) in the UK.

The RAF also adopted the Meteor TT.20, primarily for use by 3/4 and 5 CAACU (flown by civilian pilots) and 1574 (Target Facilities) Flight, a Regular RAF unit, based at Singapore.

Excluding foreign sales, forty-four NF.11/TT.20 conversions were ultimately completed for issue to British units, with twenty-five going to the RN, one to the RAE, and most of the remainder to the RAF to which a number of ex-RN examples were later transferred. Dwindling quantities remained in service into the early 1970s when they were replaced by the Canberra TT.18.

Strictly, Meteor F.4 (ex-EE545, ex-A&AEE) was never operated by the Fleet Air Arm at all, but it was allocated to the RN and despatched to RNAS Bramcote to become instructional airframe A2332 (visible aft of the fuselage roundel) on 23 October 1953. As may be seen, it carries a mix of late-war and post-war roundels and its port engine is serialed E3108. This airframe was Written off Charge (as opposed to struck off charge – no, we don't know either!) on 13 October 1955.
Newark Air Museum

The Royal Navy also made use of the Meteor T.7 as a land-based trainer obtaining at least thirty-seven of them. WL353 'HF/574' is seen at Hal Far in 1963 having acquired its overall gloss black paint scheme in 1962, possibly around the time it received a nose-mounted Harley light. WL353 was SOC on 21 November 1969.
Tony Buttler collection

T.7, WS103 'BY', in 1965 seen while held by the Aircraft Holding Unit at Brawdy, Pembrokeshire in December 1962. WS103 survives today in preservation. (See colour section)
Newark *Air Museum*

High Speed Silver overall and even devoid of T-bands, T.7, WS104 '937', seen while serving with Lossiemouth's Station Flight in 1958/59, cuts a somewhat boring figure for modellers – yet, for a time, this is how they appeared. WS104 was SOC on 18 June 1964.
Newark Air Museum

British Meteor Miscellany

Used for ejection seat trials and maintained by today's Martin-Baker Aircraft Company at Chalgrove, Oxfordshire, T.7, WA638 (G-JWMA since 4 September 2015) might also be referred to as a T.7½ due to its F.8 empennage. Powered by two Rolls-Royce Derwent 9s, as of 16 November 2016, WA638 had amassed 1,241 flying hours since being delivered from the manufacturer during November 1949: an *average* of 18.5 flying hours per year. This photograph was taken by Fred in July 2002.

The other Martin-Baker T.7½ is WL419, seen here at Chalgrove in April 1985 undergoing maintenance. We presume the yellow paint acted as a base or undercoat applied prior to the day-glo orange…

…because, as can be seen in this 1992 photo, the yellow paint is beginning to reappear as WL419's orange day-glo begins to thin or fade. *Both: Fred Martin collection*

In February 1952 NF.11, WD604, undertook trials at the A&AEE with two 100-gallon wingtip tanks. No problems were encountered and the fuel tanks fed and jettisoned without difficulty. Unusually, the tanks were fitted with fins positioned near the front rather than the rear and had a 10° incidence to help push them away from the airframe when released. *Tony Buttler collection*

NF.11, WD686, seen in September 1965, was used in the development of AI radar. *Tony Buttler collection*

Built as an NF.11, WD790 later received an NF.12 tail and unofficially became a hybrid NF.11½. Seen at Finningley in September 1970, WD790 was operated by the Radar Research Establishment for various trials including the testing of radar intended for TSR.2. *Fred Martin collection*

All-black NF.11, WM232, was used in connection with 'Blue-Jay' infra-red air-to-air missile tests – or at least was used to test the missile's seeker head by becoming a target. While WM232 was scrapped in November 1958, Blue Jay, in its fully developed form went on to become 'Firestreak', Britain's first operational guided air-to-air missile.
Tony Buttler collection

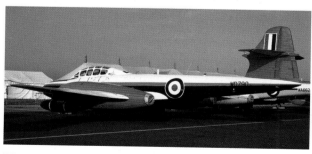

WD790 was transferred to RAE Bedford in April 1977 and subsequently received the famed RAE 'Raspberry Ripple' colour scheme, making WD790 unique as it wasn't applied to any other Meteor. Seen in July 1981, it was broken up a year later as a source of spares for the ill-fated CFS Meteor(s). *Fred Martin collection*

Carrying the A&AEE's motif on its fin, NF.14, WS838, was operated by that unit until 1969, latterly in a photo-chase capacity. It transferred to RAE Bedford where it continued to fly until February 1972 when it was flown into preservation at Colerne Museum, which must have been the last flight of a British-operated NF.14. *Via Tony Buttler*

CEV Flight Test Centre Meteors

Below: NF.11, 'NF11-1', seen at the *Centre d'Essais en Vol* (CEV), Brétigny-sur-Orge in August 1976.
Fred Martin collection

Although France purchased quantities of Meteors, all, sadly, lie beyond the confines of this book. However! During the 1970s and 1980s, Fred Martin visited the CEV at Brétigny-sur-Orge, France, and took several photos which are included here as their quality was too enticing to ignore, and it presents modellers with the opportunity to consider other possibilities when tackling a Meteor NF.11 or NF.14 – if they can source one. Thus, we hope readers will welcome their inclusion and accept the deliberate contradiction to this volume's title.

Above left: 'NF11-1', seen at Brétigny years later in September 1982 displaying small changes in appearance.

Above: NF.11, 'NF11 Nº 3', is seen at Brétigny in September 1980. (See colour section)

Left: NF.11, 'BG' No.8, at Brétigny in July 1981. The single numeral '8' can be seen near the top of the fin and on the nosewheel door.
All: Fred Martin collection

Above: NF.11, 'BF' No.9 in September 1982.

Upper right: NF.11, 'BV' No.14 at an unknown location in July 1985.

Lower right: Having previously served with the RAF as WS747, France obtained it in August 1955 for the CEV as NF14-747. A second NF.14, WS796, was obtained for the CEV in October 1955 to become NF14-796. This image dates from June 1976, but by September 1982, 747, had acquired day-glo on the upper half of its fin with 747 applied just below the fin tip, while the day-glo on its nose had been moved further aft to join with the black anti-glare panel, thus covering the nosewheel door too. No prizes for guessing where the underwing tank came from! *All: Fred Martin collection*

Below: Judging by the positioning of the day-glo on its nose, and the fact that national markings are carried on its fin, it is presumed that this photograph of NF14-747 predates the previous image by several years. *Tony Buttler collection*

Meteor Camouflage and Markings

Prototypes and Service introduction

By the time design work had begun on the finalised F.9/40 in late 1941 and early 1942, the colour scheme adopted for UK/Northern European-based day fighter aircraft, under which role the Meteor fell, was the Day Fighter Scheme comprising Ocean Grey and Dark Green upper surfaces – in the A Scheme, to Pattern No 1 where the upper surface camouflage colours extend well down the fuselage sides – and Medium Sea Grey under surfaces, although the upper/under surface demarcation on the engine nacelles was on a line with the leading edge of the wing, along the centreline of the nacelle when seen in side elevation. The wing leading edges also had a Yellow identification strip applied on both wings from the wing tip to half way along the wing.

The first prototypes featured Yellow under surfaces, (rather than Medium Sea Grey) and carried the Yellow 'P' within a circle marking denoting a prototype, on the fuselage sides, but both they and the first production Meteor F.1s were all finished in the Day Fighter Scheme (Ocean Grey and Dark Green) upper surfaces with Post May 1942 style National markings.

54-inch diameter Red and Blue roundels, (officially designated as National marking Is), were carried above the mainplanes, with 32-inch diameter Red, White and Blue roundels (National marking IIs) under the mainplanes, and 36-inch diameter Red, White, Blue, Yellow roundels (National marking IIIs) on the fuselage sides. Initially, the tail fin marking (i) – aka fin flash – was 24 inches wide and 24 inches high (to comply with the standard 24-inch x 24-inch dimensions for 'Medium' aircraft), and extended onto the rudder horn balance on some of the prototypes, but, by the introduction of the first operational F.1s, the fin flash had been reduced in height and only occupied that part of the fin above the tailplane and didn't overlap onto the rudder. 8-inch-high black serial numbers were carried on the extreme rear fuselage, with all the prototypes and F.1s, and many of the early production F.3s having the suffix '/G' added to the end of the serial to signify 'Guard', indicating that the aircraft was to be guarded at all times when on the ground. Despite being non-operational, the prototype aircraft, as well as all the operational Marks, carried the Sky 18-inch-wide Fighter Command band around the rear fuselage.

When the Meteor F.1 was cleared for service use and the first production F.1s started to arrive at RAF Manston in Kent to begin re-equipping 616 Squadron in July 1944, the unit's codes 'YQ' and individual aircraft letters were applied in approximately 20-inch-high Sky characters, invariably with the individual aircraft letter repeated on the nosewheel door in black.

The first F.3s started to arrive on the Squadron in August 1944, still fitted with the Welland engine but with sliding canopy hoods, finished in the same camouflage and markings as the F.1s, and together both Marks undertook Anti-Diver (anti-V1 Flying Bomb) patrols throughout the rest of the year.

By the beginning of 1945, the invasion of Europe was sufficiently established to consider operating Meteors from bases on the Continent and as such, a detachment of four F.3s, EE235 'YQ-P', EE239 'YQ-Q', EE240 'YQ-R' and EE241 'YQ-S' were flown to B.58 Melsbroek, in Belgium, on 4 February 1945. But, mainly due to bad weather, their operations were restricted to training flights for the benefit of air and ground forces to familiarise themselves with the new jet fighter. As such, as an aid to quick identification of an unfamiliar shape, and as a precaution against being misidentified as a Luftwaffe jet, all four Meteors were painted overall white, with just the National markings and the 'last three' of the serial number being painted around. The individual aircraft letter of the nosewheel door was also retained.

Derwent-engined F.3s

As production of the Derwent engine got into stride, they were fitted to all subsequent Meteor F.3s, giving the Mark a significant increase in speed to over 490mph at 30,000ft. These improved F.3s were issued to 616 Squadron who operated them, initially out of B.77 Gilze-Rijen in Holland, and then various other airfields as they followed the retreating German army including B.91 Nijmegen also in Holland, and in to Germany itself at B.109 Quakenbrück, B.152 Fassberg, B.156 Luneberg, and at the beginning of May, B.158 Lubeck, where they stayed until the end of hostilities.

During their time on the continent, 616 Squadron's Derwent-engined F.3s retained the same standard Day Fighter Scheme and markings as the previous Welland-engined Meteor F.1s and F.3s with the exception of the upper wing roundels which were altered by adding a narrow White ring in between the Red and Blue, effectively creating a 54-inch diameter National marking II, which was officially designated as a National marking IA.

Introduced on all operational RAF aircraft in January 1945 as an additional aid to identification following some 'unfortunate incidents' involving USAAF aircraft, because of the need to replace such a large number of different sized National marking Is on the many aircraft types operated by the RAF, it was decided that the overall diameter of the aircrafts' existing roundel's Blue segment was to remain the same as before, and a narrow White ring of proportional width, which equated to 4 inches in the Meteor's case, be applied equally over where the Red and the Blue of the roundel met.

With the exception of the introduction of applying the serial number under the wings, in the Meteor's case outboard of the engine nacelles in 16-inch-high characters, in black reading from the front under the port wing and from the rear under the starboard wing, this late wartime scheme and markings were retained in the immediate post-war period.

Underwing serials were initially introduced a few weeks after the cessation of hostilities in the European and Mediterranean Theatres of Operations following a (perhaps understandable) increase in cases of exuberant, if strictly unauthorised, low flying which sadly resulted in a number of accidents endangering not only the aircraft and crew, but civilian population too.

Post-war 'camouflage' policy

Towards the end of 1945, Air Ministry Conferences were held to plan the future of the post-war RAF, amongst which were discussions about camouflage schemes and markings, at which it was decided that there should be a return to the pre-war policy of having one standard colour for most aircraft types.

Whereas the American military had opted for a generally unpainted natural metal finish for all its aircraft, the Air Ministry retained the wartime camouflage schemes for certain types such as heavy bombers and night fighters, but went for a painted Aluminium scheme applied overall, often referred to as High Speed Silver (HSS – which in fact replaced Aluminium as the specification for the glossy overall silver finish in the late 1940s), for its day fighters, which included the Meteor.

National markings initially remained the same as the late-war period, with 54-inch diameter National marking IAs above the wings, 32-inch National marking IIs below, and 36-inch diameter National marking IIIs on the fuselage sides. The tail fin marking (i) remained at 24 inches wide but only extended to the top of the fin and didn't overlap on to the rudder horn balance. Serial numbers remained at 8 inches high in black on the extreme rear fuselage, repeated under the wings outboard of the engine nacelles in 16-inch-high black characters, again reading from the front under the port wing and from the rear under the starboard wing. The Yellow wing leading edge stripes and Sky rear fuselage band were no longer applied. Squadron codes and individual aircraft letters were retained, applied in black, in approximately 20-inch-high characters. It was during this immediate post-war period and the general introduction of the overall painted Aluminium finish that squadron badges started to make an appearance, invariably positioned on the nose or the fin.

As may be appreciated, in a cash-strapped, post-war British economy, where austerity was the watchword, although new airframes were soon being manufactured in the new overall painted Aluminium scheme, for aircraft already in service, the removal of existing camouflage prior to the application of silver paint took time, and both camouflaged and silver Meteors could be seen, often within the same squadron, for many months.

Then, in late 1946 to early 1947, further discussions were undertaken regarding the re-design of the National markings, in which the Royal Aircraft Establishment (RAE) had been involved. Eventually, after a period of confusion and disagreement, a 1-2-3 proportioned roundel was adopted, in new Bright Red, White, and Bright Blue shades that contrasted with the duller wartime red and blue shades, to be carried in all six positions, (above and below the wings and on the fuselage sides), with a similarly equally proportioned bright Red, White and Bright Blue fin marking, which was adopted in March 1947. The outer diameters of the markings were the same as the wartime ones – 54-inch above the wings; 36-inch on the fuselage sides, with a slight increase to 36 from 32-inches under the wings. Again, it took

time for the new post-war National markings to be applied to in-service machines, and examples of overall painted Aluminium Meteors with a mix of wartime (in the darker, duller red and blue shades) and the brighter red and blue shade post-war style National markings was not uncommon, as were examples of camouflaged Meteors with a full set of post-war National markings.

Squadron bars/fuselage bars/fighter bars

Irrespective of what people choose to call them, from about early 1950, UK-based day fighters, including Meteor F.3s and by now the first of the F.4s, were starting to be seen with colourful rectangular bars flanking the fuselage roundel in place of squadron codes; a style of marking that was originally started in WWI, and was developed by RAF squadrons in the 1920s and 30s. Despite initial disapproval by 'higher authority' these 'squadron bars', which at first were applied unofficially, became accepted (not least because of the *esprit de corps* they engendered), and rapidly replaced squadron codes on all day fighter units and appeared on both overall Aluminium and camouflaged aircraft.

A return to camouflage

The worsening of relations and the subsequent build-up of tensions between the Soviet Bloc in the East and what became NATO (North Atlantic Treaty Organisation) members in the West after the end of World War II, resulting in what was generally referred to as the Cold War, created a perceived need to camouflage aeroplanes, especially when they were dispersed on airfields, and as such, during early the 1950s Second Tactical Air Force (2TAF) Vampire FB.5s based in Germany were the first RAF aircraft to appear in a new camouflage scheme, comprising glossy Dark Sea Grey and Dark Green upper surfaces with PRU Blue undersides to Pattern No 1.

Introduced under Air Ministry Order A658/52 in December 1952, and initially named the Long-Range Day Fighter, Ground Attack, Fighter Reconnaissance and Photo Reconnaissance Scheme, Meteor F.8s (which had been introduced in 1951), started to appear in Dark Sea Grey and Dark Green upper surfaces to Pattern No 1, albeit still retaining 'silver' under surfaces, which was now known officially as High Speed Silver (HSS) as explained in the following passage: *During WWII and the early post-war period, many RAF aircraft received a partial or overall coat of aluminium paint. In recent years confusion has arisen between the application of aluminium or silver paint. In January 1953, an internal memo AMOA.658/52, dated 18 December 1952, was circulated stating that the previously referred to colour 'Aluminium' would be referred to from that point as 'High Speed Silver' as opposed to its previous name. Later, in January 1953, a Ministry of Supply memo stated that in all such references the word silver was to replace aluminium and the words 'High Speed' were to replace 'High Gloss' which was often used as a prefix to Aluminium. Thus: same paint and finish – just another name.*

The 1-2-3 proportioned Bright Red, White and Bright Blue roundels were retained in all six positions, with the equally proportioned Bright Red, White and Bright Blue fin flash, and serial numbers remained at 8 inches high in black on the extreme rear fuselage, repeated under the wings outboard of the engine nacelles in 16-inch-high black characters. Squadron bars flanking the fuselage roundels had become the norm by the early/mid-1950s, with just an individual aircraft letter, invariably carried on the fin and often on the nosewheel door. Squadron badges, sometimes flanked by miniature reproductions of the Squadron bars could often be found on the outer faces of the engine nacelles.

RAF T.7 and F.8 in secondary roles

To help with jet-conversion training and advanced training for Meteor pilots, the two-seat T.7 trainer was developed and introduced into RAF (and Fleet Air Arm) service in the early 1950s. Initially finished in overall HSS with standard post-war 'bright' National markings, it wasn't until the mid-1950s that the T.7s adopted Yellow trainer bands ('T-bands') around the rear fuselage and across the chord of the wings, outboard of the engine nacelles, but not overlapping the ailerons. A little later, the Target Tug Scheme, of Yellow under surfaces with broad diagonal Black stripes (to Pattern No 1) was introduced on many station flight T.7s. On both squadron-operated and station flight T.7s, squadron bars were frequently carried, those on the station flight machines often reflecting the various squadrons stationed there.

F.8s were also utilised in the training role, being allocated to OCUs, CAACUs and target facilities flights both at home and abroad. Generally retaining their original basic 'operational' schemes – either overall HSS, or Dark Sea Grey and Dark Green upper surfaces with HSS under surfaces.

Following the demise of Yellow T-bands from the early 1960s, bright orange day-glo was introduced, initially in paint form applied to solid areas of the airframe, but later in the form of pre-prepared adhesive strips applied to the rear fuselage, nose, engine nacelles and wing tips. Additionally, when F.8s were used in the TT role, the Target Tug Scheme, of Yellow under surfaces with broad diagonal Black stripes (to Pattern No 1) was applied.

Photo Recce Meteors

Two Marks of Meteor were used in the Photo Reconnaissance role – FR.9s and PR.10s. Based upon the F.8 but fitted with a pressurised and heated camera bay in the nose which extended the fuselage length by 9ins, the FR.9s were initially finished in overall HSS with bright National markings in all positions. However, they soon acquired camouflage in the form of the 2nd Tactical Air Forces' Long Range Day Fighter, Ground Attack, Fighter Reconnaissance and Photo Reconnaissance Scheme, comprising Dark Sea Grey and Dark Green upper surfaces with PRU Blue under surfaces to Pattern No 1, although some airframes retained HSS under surfaces. Bright Red, White, Bright Blue National markings were carried in all positions with black serials on the rear fuselage, which were repeated under the wings. Squadron bars, were later applied to either side of the fuselage roundel, with the individual aircraft letter usually to be found on the fin and nosewheel door.

Conversely, some FR.9s were finished in the High Altitude Short Range Day Fighter Scheme, comprising Light Slate Grey and Medium Sea Grey upper surfaces with PRU Blue under surfaces to Pattern No 2, (i.e. with the upper/under surface colours demarcation high up the fuselage sides). Again, Bright Red, White, Bright Blue national markings were carried in all positions, with black serial numbers on the rear fuselage, which were repeated under the wings and

squadron bars either side of the fuselage roundel.

The Meteor PR.10, unlike the FR.9, was unarmed but had a camera fitted in its nose with two others in the rear fuselage pointing downwards. Initially finished in overall HSS, with national markings in all positions and black serial numbers on the rear fuselage and under the wings, several airframes were repainted in the High Altitude Photo Reconnaissance Scheme – more usually seen on early PR Canberras – comprising Medium Sea Grey upper surfaces over PRU Blue undersides to Pattern No 2.

Meteor Night Fighters

In early 1950, RAF night fighters (namely the Mosquito NF.36) were still finished in the wartime overall Medium Sea Grey with Dark Green disruptive upper surfaces, albeit with post-war National markings in the 'bright' Red and Blue colours. As such, Meteor NF.11s were finished in the same scheme, with post-war National markings above the wings, on the fuselage sides and on the fin, again in the 'bright' Red and Blue colours. Squadron bars were applied to Fighter Command NF.11s from the outset in most cases, as the squadrons themselves either reformed or re-equipped with the type commencing August 1951. However, the four 2TAF squadrons initially carried code letters until replaced by fuselage bars from 1953 into 1954.

The Meteor NF.13s, which entered RAF service in 1953, were also initially finished in the 'wartime' overall Medium Sea Grey with Dark Green disruptive upper surfaces.

Following major servicing and/or refurbishment several surviving NF.11s were repainted in the Dark Sea Grey and Dark Green upper surfaces and Light Aircraft Grey undersides scheme, as too was at least one NF.13; was there more than one? Following the change in camouflage, fuselage serials were generally re-applied in white.

As with the previous Night Fighter Marks, NF.12s, were initially delivered in the overall Medium Sea Grey with Dark Green disruptive pattern upper surfaces Night Fighter Scheme, with 'bright' National markings and squadron bars flanking the fuselage roundels, but, after major servicing and/or refurbishment some of them were also repainted in the Dark Sea Grey and Dark Green upper surfaces and Light Aircraft Grey undersides scheme with white fuselage serial numbers.

The last Meteor night fighter, the NF.14, essentially an NF.12, finally dispensed with the heavily framed canopy inherited from its Meteor T.7 origins, and featured a clear, one-piece 'blown' canopy hood, that afforded the crew a superb all-around view.

The NF.14s were finished in the Dark Sea Grey and Dark Green upper surfaces and Light Aircraft Grey undersides from the start, but with the demarcation between the upper and under surface colours on the fuselage sides initially set at the same mid-way level as per the previous overall Medium Sea Grey and Dark Green scheme. Fuselage serial numbers were black. However, at some later point, possibly following major servicing or refurbishment, the upper surface demarcation was lowered to effectively match Pattern No 1, and white fuselage serial numbers were applied. An initial feature of the NF.14's Dark Sea Grey/Dark Green/Light Aircraft Grey scheme was that the fin and rudder under the level of the tailplane was finished in the under-surface Light Aircraft Grey, with just the section of fin and rudder above the tailplane in the Dark Sea Grey/Dark Green. However, presumably following major servicing or refurbishment, it is thought by the MUs or Aircraft Servicing Flights, the upper surface camouflage colours were applied to the whole of the fin and rudder, both above and below the level of the tailplane.

Royal Navy Meteors

Two Meteor F.3s, EE337 and EE387, powered by uprated Derwent 5 engines were adapted for carrier trials to investigate issues arising from operating jets at sea. Finished in the then standard Fleet Air Arm scheme of Extra Dark Sea Grey upper surfaces with Sky undersides to Pattern No 2, post-war 1-2-3 proportioned roundels in the 'bright' colours were carried in all six positions. The serial number and ROYAL NAVY legend were applied in 4-inch-high characters at the extreme rear of the fuselage, and a three-digit code on the fuselage sides, just to the rear of the roundels (e.g. '051' on EE337, with the RNAS Station code 'FD' for RNAS Ford on the fin, all in black.

The operational trials took place aboard HMS *Implacable* and included carrier landings after which the two aircraft moved ashore to RNAS Ford with 778 Carrier Trials Squadron.

Fleet Air Arm T.7 trainers

The Meteor also entered Royal Navy service as a land-based trainer. Early naval jet aircraft, such as the de Havilland Sea Vampire, Sea Venom and Hawker Sea Hawk, were sufficiently different to piston-engined aircraft that the RN realised that a two-seater trainer would be essential, so the RAF's T.7 variant was quickly adopted to give FAA pilots shore-based experience in jet aircraft handling, before flying other jet aircraft.

Initially finished identically to their RAF counterparts in the overall HSS scheme, with post-war roundels but no fin flashes, the serial number and ROYAL NAVY legend were initially applied 4 inches high in black at the extreme rear of the fuselage, but later the ROYAL NAVY legend was sometimes moved further forward and applied in 8-inch high characters, just to the rear of the fuselage roundels. A three-digit code number was also carried, invariably in black, either on the nose or on the fuselage sides just to the rear of the roundels. Sometimes this copied the 'last three' of the serial, but not always. The RN Air Base code, 'FD' for Ford (up to November 1958 when it was de-commissioned), and 'CW' (up to 1953) then 'CU' for Culdrose, were usually applied to fin.

Yellow, and then later, day-glo, T-bands were applied on the nose, rear fuselage and wings of many of the Royal Navy's T.7s, which ultimately morphed into the day-glo adhesive strips towards the end of the surviving T.7s service lives with the RN. Also, at some point, some of the last surviving T.7s were given an overall gloss black scheme, (similar to, but pre-dating by many years, the 'Longview 2' air-to-air visibility scheme adopted by the RAF and FAA for the BAe Hawk T.1s in 1992), resulting in the serial numbers, ROYAL NAVY legend and air base codes being applied in white. Roundels remained in the usual six positions in the 'bright' colours. The last two RN T.7s (other than WS103) were SOC in November 1969.

TT.20: Royal Navy

The TT.20 was a dedicated target towing aircraft created by modifying surplus NF.11s. RN examples were finished in the overall HSS scheme, with 'bright' post-war roundels in six positions, their undersides utilising the Target Tug Yellow and Black diagonal band scheme.

However, the RN adopted the paler Saturn Yellow for its target tugs, as opposed to the RAF's standard Yellow as this section from Air Publication 119A-0600-1, Aircraft Surface Finishes and Markings states: 'Scheme for Meteor TT.20 aircraft. Fluorescent Red-Orange is not suitable for use on this aircraft as the targets which it tows are of this colour. To ensure satisfactory distinction the existing colour scheme for this aircraft is to be retained with the exception that Saturn Yellow is to be applied where standard Yellow markings are at present used.'

Yellow T-bands were applied around the rear fuselage and above the wings, which it seems the TT.20s retained to the end, without their ever having made much use, if any, of solid day-glo bands or adhesive strips.

RN serial numbers were in black 4-inch-high characters, sometimes positioned on the base of the fin, which were later re-applied on the fuselage in 8-inch-high characters. 'ROYAL NAVY' appeared on the rear fuselage A three-digit number, sometimes the 'last three' of the serial number, though not always, was carried on the nose, with the RN air base code on the fin. The ML Aviation Type G winch was overall Yellow (with black windmill blades), the shade used dependant presumably upon the under-surface colour – as too did the drop tanks.

TT.20: RAF

The RAF made significant use of the Meteor TT.20, primarily with 3/4 and 5 CAACU (flown by civilian pilots at Exeter and Woodvale respectively), to which should be added 1574 (Target Facilities) Flight a Regular RAF unit based at Singapore. All appear to have been finished in HSS with the Target Tug Golden Yellow and Black diagonal band under surfaces scheme. 'Bright' post-war roundels were applied in six positions and most were normally to be seen carrying Yellow underwing tanks often with silver-painted upper halves. Unlike their naval counterparts, RAF TT.20s made extensive use of solid orange bands, and later adhesive day-glo strips on the rear fuselage, nose, wings and engine nacelles.

Unmanned Target Drones

Finished in an overall Signal Red scheme with Yellow upper surfaces, essentially to Pattern No 2, post-war National markings were carried in all positions, with the fin flash narrowly outlined in white, and the serial number applied on the fuselage sides in black. The wingtip camera pods were also black. Most of these aircraft were delivered to the Woomera Weapons Research Establishment in Australia from 1955, however, twenty or so were delivered to RAF Llanbedr in North Wales, making their first flights over Cardigan Bay in July 1958, and a small number went to 728B NAS, at Hal Far, Malta.

As the number of U.15s began to dwindle, a similar number of Meteor F.8s were converted to unmanned target drones and designated as U.16s (later D.16s). Colour scheme and markings were the same as the U.15s, and by this time, both the remaining U.15s and the U.16s, carried an individual aircraft letter in Yellow on the fin under the tailplanes, which was repeated, also in Yellow, on the nosewheel door.

Gloster F.9/40, DG202/G, Gloster Aircraft Company's airfield, Hucclecote, Gloucestershire, mid-1944 | Although DG202 was the first F.9/40, it was not the first 'Meteor' to fly, that privilege going to DG206, however it did take to the air on 24 July 1943 and was later used for deck handling tests aboard aircraft carrier HMS *Pretoria Castle*. Finished in the Day Fighter Scheme of Ocean Grey and Dark Green upper surfaces with Yellow under surfaces, the aircraft carried the Yellow 'P' within a circle denoting a prototype, and the suffix 'G' added to its serial to signify 'Guard', indicating that it was to be guarded at all times when on the ground. Of interest is the lack of the 'acorn' fairing on the leading edge of the fin. Despite being non-operational, the aircraft carried the Sky 18-inch-wide Day Fighter band around the rear fuselage. Also, note the way in which the fin flash extends onto the rudder horn balance to ensure a dimension of 24 x 24 inches.

Meteor F.1, EE228 'XL-P', 1335 Conversion Unit, RAF Molesworth, Cambridgeshire, summer 1946 | The first unit formally intended to train fighter pilots on the jet-powered Meteor was 1335 CU, which arrived at RAF Molesworth, on 27 July 1945, flying a mix of Meteor F.1s and F.3s. EE228, one of a batch of twenty Meteor F.1s delivered between February and September 1944, had previously served with 616 Squadron, and was still finished in the wartime Day Fighter Scheme, with Medium Sea Grey under surfaces and wartime National markings, and carried the unit code 'XL' allocated to 1335 CU which later became 226 OCU.

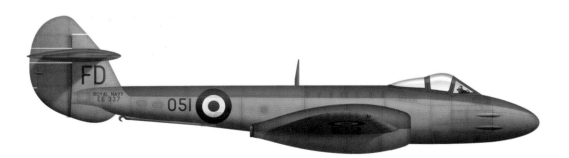

Meteor F.3, EE337 '051/FD', 703 Naval Air Squadron, RNAS Lea-on-Solent, Hampshire, June 1948 | Built as a standard Meteor F.3, EE337 was converted by Gloster Aircraft and fitted with an A-frame arrester hook off a DH Sea Hornet and was re-engined with uprated Derwent 5s. It was also fitted with an improved braking system and strengthened fuselage and undercarriage for deck landing trials. The aircraft made the first landing by a twin-engined jet on an aircraft carrier, HMS *Implacable*. Finished in the then standard FAA scheme of Extra Dark Sea Grey upper surfaces and Sky undersides to Pattern No 2, it carried the recently introduced 'post-war' 1-2-3 dimensioned roundels, the fuselage code '051' and the RNAS Station code 'FD' for RNAS Ford. It was eventually struck off charge in October 1956.

Meteor F.3, EE286 'MR-Q', 245 Squadron, RAF Colerne, Wiltshire, summer 1945 | Re-formed from elements of 504 Squadron which had disbanded in August 1945, with many of the pilots and the Meteor F.3s of that unit, 245 was among the immediate post-war Fighter Command squadrons to operate the F.3. EE286 had previously served with 504 Squadron, but had been re-coded with 245 Squadron codes and was still finished in the wartime Day Fighter Scheme of Ocean Grey and Dark Green – in the A Scheme, to Pattern No 1 where the upper surface camouflage colours extend well down the fuselage sides – and Medium Sea Grey under surfaces, with wartime-style National markings.

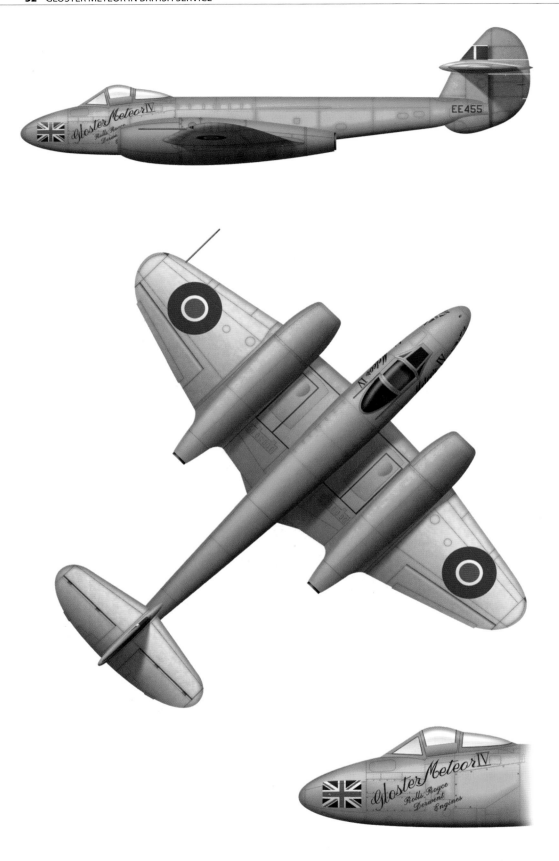

Meteor F.4, EE455 'Forever Amber', from the RAF's High-Speed Flight, November 1945 | Ordered as a Meteor F.3, EE455, 'Forever Amber' (often referred to as the 'Yellow Peril') was completed as an F.4 and allocated to the High-Speed Flight along with Meteor EE454, 'Britannia', for high speed trials prior to making an attempt on the World Air Speed Record. The attempt was made on 7 November 1945, with EE455 completing the 3km course at 603mph, while EE454 achieved a new air speed record of 606.25mph. For the attempt, EE455 was given a high-gloss yellow colour scheme, but with polished natural metal outer wing panels, tailplane and elevators with wartime-style National markings restricted to the wings and fin. EE455 was SOC on 1 January 1954.

Meteor F.4, VW300 'X', of 600 (City of London) Squadron, RAF Biggin Hill, Kent, late 1951 | Finished in the post-war Day Fighter Scheme of overall painted Aluminium* introduced in 1947, VW300 is illustrated sporting the Squadron's bars. The interlocking red and white triangles flanking the fuselage roundel was a style of marking originally used by RAF squadrons in the 1920s and 30s which was gradually being reintroduced in the early 1950s and replacing squadron codes following the change-over from the dull wartime camouflage. The Squadron badge, an RAF golden eagle over a St George's shield and blue scroll with '600' and 'City of London Squadron' in gold, flanked by miniature bars, was displayed below the cockpit. Of interest is the mix of wartime and post-war National markings – a relatively common occurrence during the late 1940s/early 1950s.

(The colour Aluminium was renamed High Speed Silver [HSS] by Ministry order – 14 December 1952)

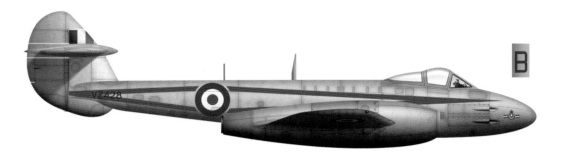

Meteor F.4, VZ428 'B', 1 Squadron, RAF Tangmere, Kent, 1950 | Finished in the post-war Day Fighter Scheme of overall Aluminium (HSS) with full post-war National markings, VZ428 was one of at least two 1 Squadron F.4s to have red, elongated stripes applied on the fuselage extending the full length from nose to rudder post, apparently when fighter squadrons were competing for entry at the RAF Display that year. The Squadron badge was carried on the nose, flanked by the unit's more familiar white bars outlined in red, with the individual aircraft letter, also in red, on the nosewheel door.

Meteor T.7, WF769 'Q', 66 Squadron, RAF Acklington, Northumberland, September 1958 | Despite having operated various Marks of Meteor in the Day Fighter role from the late 1940s through to the early-1950s, by 1958, 66 Squadron was equipped with Hunter F.6s, but kept several Meteor T.7s on strength for pilot appraisal, instrument rating and continuity training. In the overall HSS scheme and carrying Yellow trainer bands around the wings and the rear fuselage, WF769 also had 66 Squadron's white bars outlined in Royal Blue flanking the fuselage roundels. The aircraft letter on the fin was also blue.

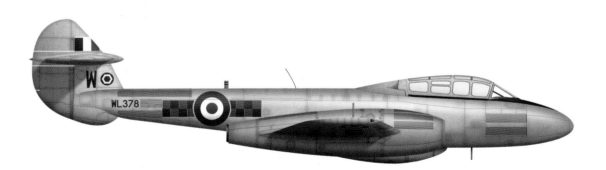

Meteor T.7, WL378 'W', 85 Squadron, RAF Binbrook, Lincolnshire, April 1968 | Upon re-forming on 1 April 1963, having previously been equipped with Javelin FAW.8s in the all-weather fighter role, 85 Squadron moved to Binbrook with a mixture of Canberras and Gloster Meteors in the Target Facilities role. Finished in the overall HSS scheme, with post-war National markings, WL378 had day-glo strips on the nose, engine nacelles and rear fuselage, together with the Squadron's red/black chequered bars flanking the fuselage roundels. The unit's white hexagon on a black disc was carried on the fin together with its black aircraft letter.

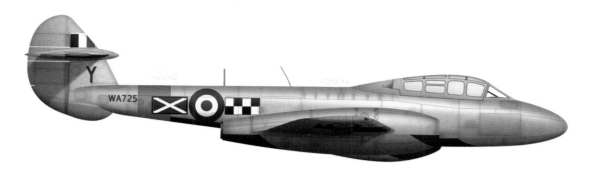

Meteor T.7, WA725 'Y', Leuchars Station Flight, RAF Leuchars, Fife, September 1958 | Most RAF Stations had a Station Flight to provide second line support for TT, continuity training and general 'hack' duties etc. Finished in overall HSS with Yellow and Black striped 'Target Tug' under surfaces, fluorescent orange wingtips and band around the rear fuselage, WA725 combined the chequers of 43 Squadron with the saltire of 151 Squadron on its fuselage bars. On 10 September 1959, WA725 was transferred to 151 Squadron, still coded 'Y', where it remained until August 1961 when it was sent to a MU prior to being scrapped in late 1962.

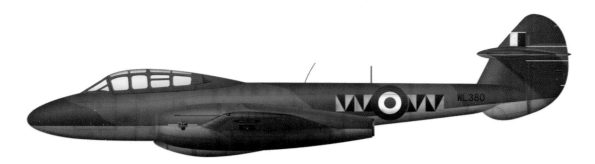

Meteor T.7, WL380, 74 Squadron, RAF Horsham St Faith, Norfolk, 1954 | 74 Squadron was based at Horsham St Faith for thirteen years from October 1946, during eleven of which it flew various Marks of Meteors, including this T.7 which it used in the mid-1950s while primarily equipped with F.8s. Originally delivered in HSS with Yellow 'T-bands', at some point in 1954, WL380 had Dark Sea Grey and Dark Green upper surfaces added to match the unit's camouflaged Meteor F.8s. The aircraft carries the unit's black and yellow segmented fuselage bars, which were presumably in the process of being added on the outer faces of the engine nacelles flanking the tiger's head.

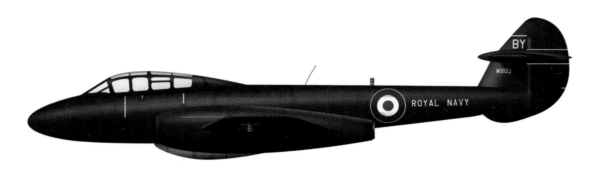

Meteor T.7, WS103 'BY', Aircraft Holding Unit, RNAS Brawdy, Pembrokeshire, late 1962 | WS103, one of thirty-seven Meteor T.7s delivered to the Royal Navy, was used for jet conversion training, communications and Station Flight duties. Having previously served with 703 and 728 NASs and various other second line units, at home and at Hal Far, Malta, by December 1962, WS103 had acquired an overall gloss black FAA Trainer scheme and was with the Aircraft Holding Unit, at Brawdy on the south-west coast of Wales. It later acquired fluorescent day-glo rear fuselage, fin and outer wing panels, and a nose light, possibly when serving with the Fleet Requirements Unit in the late 1960s/early 1970s, and ended up in the FAA Museum before moving to Cobham Hall in December 1999.

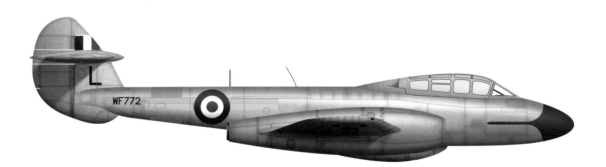

Meteor T.7, WF772 'L', 208 Squadron, Ta' Qali, Malta, September 1957 | At this time, 208 Squadron was still equipped with the Meteor FR.9 with one or more T.7s on strength. Finished in the overall HSS scheme, as well as Yellow trainer bands around the rear fuselage and wings, WF772 had 208 Squadron's light blue and yellow bars flanking its fuselage roundels and a nose flash in Blue Flight's colour. WF772 went on to serve with Malta's Communication & Target Towing Squadron, prior to joining 29 Squadron (Javelins) in Cyprus before ending its days on Leuchars' fire dump in May 1968.

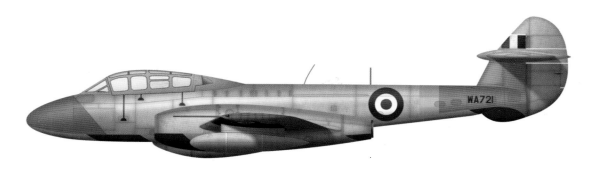

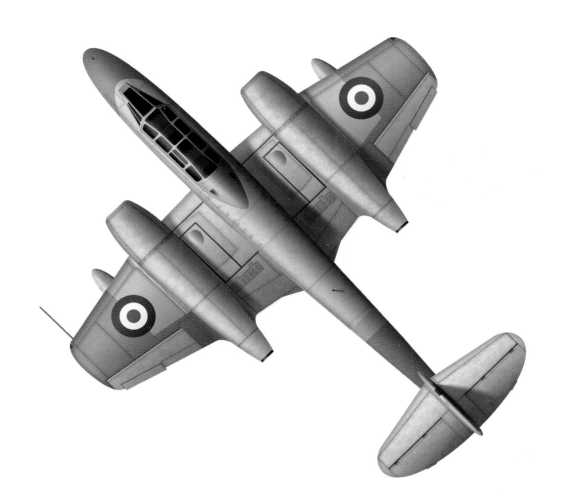

Meteor T.7, WA721, 74 Squadron, RAF Coltishall, Norfolk, 1963 | Having served with 501 and 23 Squadrons, by mid-1963 WA721 was with 74 Squadron when it was equipped with some of the first Lightning F.1s. Finished in overall HSS and Yellow and Black striped 'Target Tug' under surface scheme, with Yellow T-bands around the mainplanes and rear fuselage, WA721 appears to be unusual in that fluorescent orange was applied over the existing T-bands, thus reducing the width of the fuselage band and abbreviating those on the upper surface outer wing panels.

Meteor F.8, WA874 '4D-K', 74 Squadron, RAF Horsham St Faith, Norfolk, early 1950s | Pre-dating the period and schemes of the 74 Squadron Meteor T.7s on the previous two pages, WA874 was still carrying squadron codes ('4D-K') revealing how it looked in the early 1950s before the introduction of fuselage bars. Finished in the overall Aluminium (HSS) Fighter scheme, WA874 spent its entire service life with 'The Tigers' from September 1950 until 5 April 1957, after which it spent its last days in storage before being ignominiously sold for scrap in July 1959.

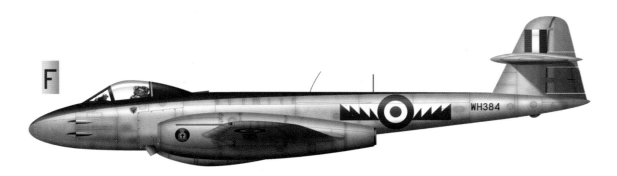

Meteor F.8, WH384 'F', 610 (County of Chester) Squadron, RAF Hooton Park, Cheshire, early 1950s | Finished in the overall Aluminium Day Fighter Scheme, WH384 had the then newly introduced squadron bars flanking the fuselage roundels applied – in 610's case, black and white diagonally divided serrations. The Squadron badge, a wheatsheaf on a black disc, was also carried on the outer faces of the engine nacelles, and the individual aircraft letter 'F' on the nosewheel door. Tragically, WH384 was lost, together with WH383, on 14 November 1953, when both aircraft flew into a hill in cloud near Edgeworth, Lancashire, killing both pilots.

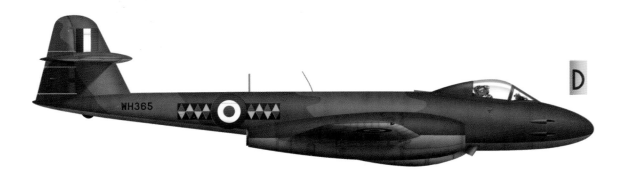

Meteor F.8, WH365 'D', 611 Squadron, RAF Hooton Park, Cheshire, mid-1950s | Also resident at RAF Hooton Park, where it joined 610 Squadron in March 1952 until both units were disbanded in February 1957, 611 (West Lancashire) Squadron's Meteor F.8s featured black fuselage bars with half-red/half-yellow diamonds displayed alternately. By the mid-1950s, there was a general trend back to camouflage for all RAF Day Fighters and WH365 was finished in Dark Sea Grey and Dark Green upper surfaces but retained the HSS under surfaces. WH365 went on to serve with 600 and 615 Squadrons before being converted into a D.16 unmanned target drone in March 1960.

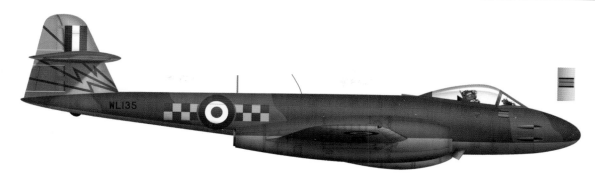

Meteor F.8, WL135, 245 Squadron, RAF Stradishall, Suffolk, July 1955 | In February 1955, WL135, originally coded 'E', was adopted as the mount of the unit's CO, Squadron Leader N K Bowen, and together with the blue and yellow chequered bars flanking the fuselage roundels, had a yellow fin and rudder applied with blue lightning flashes. In addition to the Squadron Leader's pennant either side of the cockpit, a third was applied to the nosewheel door in lieu of an individual aircraft letter. Finished in the new Day Fighter Scheme of Dark Sea Grey and Dark Green upper surfaces with HSS undersides, WL135 remained with 245 Squadron until sold for scrap in May 1959.

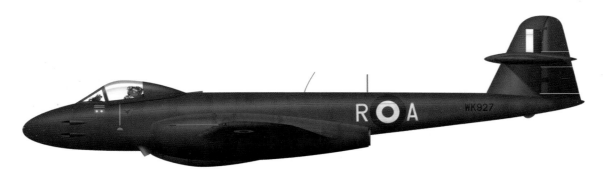

Meteor F.8, WK927 'R-A', 12 Group Communications Flight, RAF Coltishall, Norfolk, flown by AVM Sir Richard Atcherley, 1953 | Allocated to 12 Group's Communications Flight, WK927 was 'adopted' by the Air Officer Commanding 12 Group, Air Vice Marshal R L Atcherley, for his personal use, hence the white R-A codes flanking the fuselage roundel. Finished in a non-standard overall semi-gloss Dark Green scheme it also featured an AVM rank pennant with dark blue edges and wide and narrow red stripes on a light blue field above an AVM's star plate (an AVM is a two-star Air Officer rank) under the windscreen. By 1955, WK927 had received a full clear-view canopy but the 'R-A' letters had been removed. It was sold for scrap in July 1959.

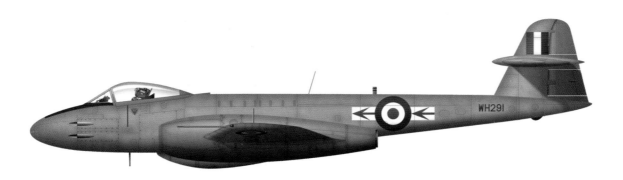

Meteor F.8, WH291, 229 OCU, RAF Chivenor, Devon, 1970s. | 229 OCU, was allocated the 'shadow' identity of 79 Squadron hence the latter's rectangular white bars with forward-pointing arrows flanking the fuselage roundel. 229 OCU maintained a handful of Meteors to provide target facilities for the unit's resident Hunters. At the time, WH291 was finished in overall Light Aircraft Grey with post-war national markings in all positions.

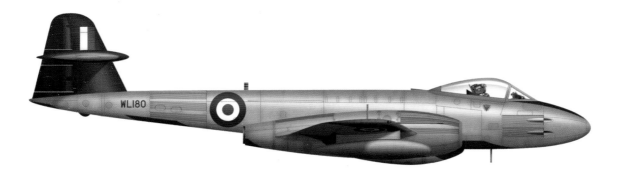

Meteor F.8, WL180, 1574 (Target Facilities) Flight, RAF Changi, Singapore, June 1969 | Formed in May 1964, 1574 (Target Facilities) Flight was equipped with a mix of Meteor T.7s, TT.20s and F.8s to tow targets for Tengah-based Hunters and Lightnings. Finished in the HSS scheme on the upper surfaces with Target Tug Yellow and Black diagonal striped under surfaces, and national markings in all positions, WL180 also had day-glo adhesive strips on the nose, rear fuselage and engine nacelles, and a gloss black fin and rudder, including the bullet fairing. It was transferred to the Royal Navy in July 1971 but its subsequent fate is unknown.

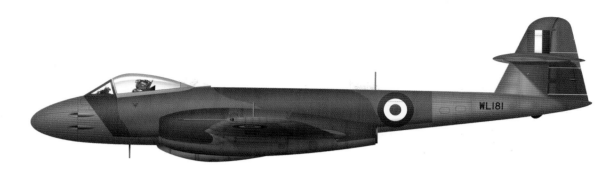

Meteor F.8, WL181, RAF Flying College/College of Air Warfare, Aerobatic Team, RAF Manby, Lincolnshire, early 1960s | The RAFFC (or RAFCAW as it became in July 1962), was an advanced flying school for experienced pilots to further their skills. Operating Meteors of various Marks, three Meteor F.8s were selected to form the College's aerobatic team, WL181 being one of them. Finished in the Dark Sea Grey/Dark Green upper surfaces with HSS undersides, the nose, rear fuselage and lower portion of the fin, and the outer wing panels, although not the ailerons, were painted in day-glo orange. Of note are the yellow wing walkway warning lines, outlining the main undercarriage bays and the smaller than usual roundels above the wings.

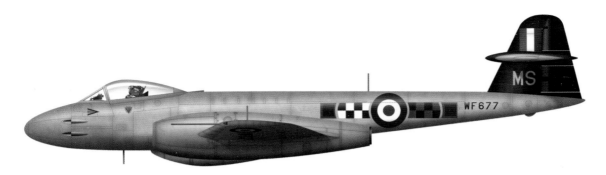

Meteor F.8, WF677 'MS', Church Fenton Wing, RAF Church Fenton, North Yorkshire, October 1957 | By October 1957 Church Fenton hosted, amongst other units, the Meteor NF.12s/14s of 72 and 85 Squadrons. WF677, the mount of the Wing Leader (W/Cdr Maurice Shaw – note the pennant), was finished in overall HSS with a black fin and rudder and the letters 'MS' in yellow on the fin. Its fuselage markings represented 72 Squadron (blue with red borders), 85 Squadron (red and black chequers) and 19 Squadron (blue and white chequers – and by now equipped with the Hunter F.6). WF677 spent its entire life with the Church Fenton Station Flight until scrapped on 5 February 1959.

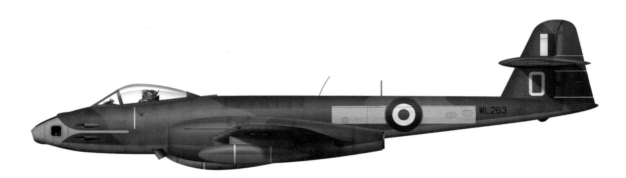

Meteor FR.9, WL263 'O', 208 Squadron, RAF Ta' Qali, Malta, August 1956 | Based at Malta by August 1956, the unit's FR.9s had by then acquired camouflage: namely the Tactical Air Forces' Long Range Day Fighter, Ground Attack, Fighter Reconnaissance and Photo Reconnaissance Scheme, introduced in December 1952, comprising Dark Sea Grey and Dark Green upper surfaces with PRU Blue under surfaces to Pattern No 1. Bright Red, White, Bright Blue National markings were carried in all positions with black serials on the rear fuselage and under the wings. The Squadron's colours, of pale blue and yellow horizontal bars, were applied to either side of the fuselage roundel, with a yellow nose flash around the camera ports (denoting 'B' Flight). The aircraft letter 'O' on the fin was white.

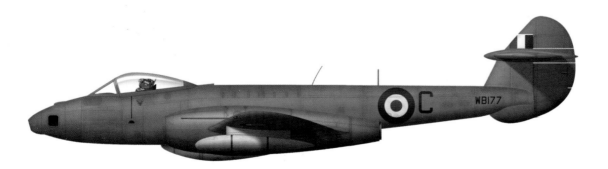

Meteor PR.10, WB177 'C', 13 Squadron, RAF Akrotiri, Cyprus, early 1956 | The Meteor PR.10, employed in the high-altitude strategic reconnaissance role, combined an F.3's wings with the fin/rudder of an F.4, centre fuselage of the F.8, and an FR.9's nose. Unarmed, it carried an F.24 camera in the nose with two F.52 cameras in the rear fuselage. Some of 13 squadron's PR.10s were painted in the High Altitude Photo Reconnaissance Scheme – more usually seen on early PR Canberras – comprising Medium Sea Grey upper surfaces over PRU Blue undersides to Pattern No 2, as shown here. Bright National markings were carried in all positions, with black serial number on the rear fuselage, repeated under the wings, and a black aircraft letter 'C' aft of the fuselage roundel.

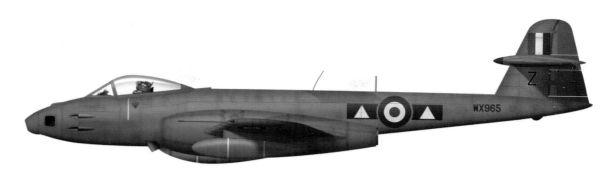

Meteor FR.9, WX965 'Z', 2 Squadron, RAF Geilenkirchen, West Germany, late 1955/early 1956 | Delivered from March 1950, FR.9s were used operationally by 2 and 79 Squadrons 2TAF in West Germany and 208 Squadron in the Middle East. Coded 'Z' on the fin in black thinly outlined in white, WX965 was one of the few FR.9s to be finished in the High Altitude Short Range Day Fighter Scheme, comprising Light Slate Grey and Medium Sea Grey upper surfaces with PRU Blue under surfaces to Pattern No 2, i.e. high up the fuselage sides. Bright Red, White, Bright Blue national markings were carried in all positions, with a black serial number on the rear fuselage which was repeated under the wings. The Squadron's black bars with white triangles flanked the fuselage roundel, while the blue-tipped fin bullet denoted it as a 'B' Flight machine.

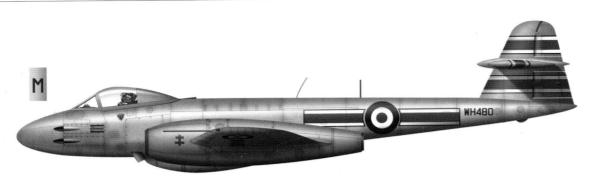

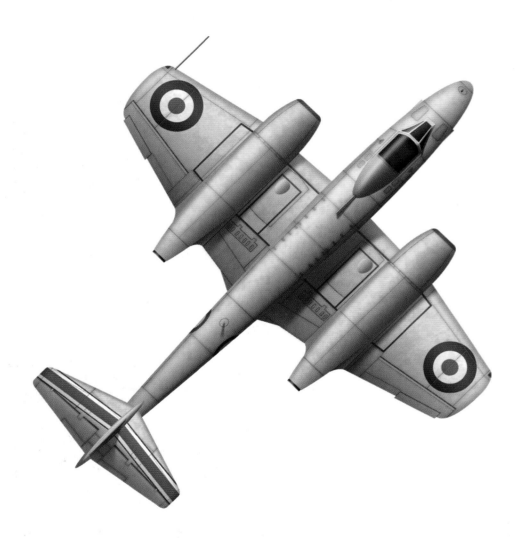

Meteor F.8, WH480 'M', 41 Squadron, RAF Biggin Hill, Kent, 1952, flown by the CO Sqn Ldr John M 'Dusty' Miller | One of the most striking liveries displayed on a Meteor must surely be that applied to Miller's personal mount, WH480, when he was CO of 41 Squadron in the early 1950s. Finished in the overall HSS scheme it had white/red/white rectangular bars thinly outlined in black flanking the fuselage roundels, across fin and rudder, and above and below the tailplane, with the unit's Arms of St. Omer cross on the outer faces of the engine intake, whose lips were also painted red. A Squadron Leader's pennant was carried below the cockpit (on both sides) and the individual aircraft letter 'M' on the nosewheel door in black.

Meteor F.4, EE521 (incorrectly coded 'VG-FG'), Central Gunnery School, RAF Leconfield, East Yorkshire, late 1950 | EE521 was allocated to the CGS at Leconfield which was created to train air gunnery instructors. Finished in the overall Aluminium (HSS) scheme with post-war National markings, it carried the four-letter Training and Reserve Command codes introduced in the spring of 1946. Allocated the codes FJR to FJX inclusive, the intention was that the three-letter unit code would appear together while the fourth, the individual aircraft letter, would be separated by the fuselage roundel. Why EE521 is coded 'VG-FJ' instead of the correct 'FJV-G' is unknown, although several other CGS machines were similarly incorrectly marked. EE521 was eventually converted into a drone and sent to Australia in January 1956.

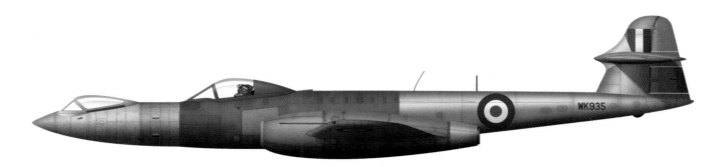

Prone Pilot Position Meteor F.8, WK935, Armstrong Whitworth facility, Baginton, Warwickshire, February 1955 | A standard Meteor F.8 airframe, WK935, was modified with a new nose section attached at the nosewheel bulkhead as part of the research into the Bristol Type 185 rocket-powered delta which was to accommodate the pilot in the prone position. This F.8 carried a second pilot lying on a couch with offset control column and suspended rear rudder pedals in the extended nose section to evaluate the effects of acceleration and inertia-induced forces while flying in a prone position, although WK935 was never flown solo from the radically altered front cockpit.

WK935 first flew in this form on 10 February 1955. It is illustrated as it is thought to have then looked with a natural metal new nose section (revealing the new panel details), various shades of primer on the mid-fuselage and engine nacelles, and what is thought to be a standard F.8 rear fuselage and tailplane in HSS with shiny natural metal leading-edge fin extensions above and below the tailplane bullet fairing covering part of the fin flash. WK935 subsequently flew another ninety-nine sorties, amassing a total of 55 flying hours before it was put into store when the Bristol 185 project was cancelled and at the time of writing resides at the RAF Museum Cosford.

Photograph of WK935. *Courtesy of Tony Buttler*

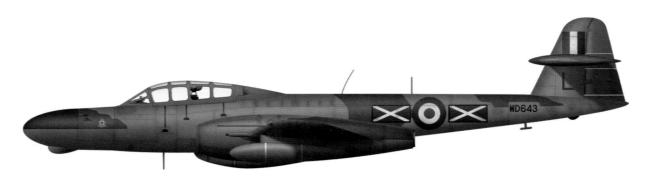

Meteor NF.11, WD643 'L', 151 Squadron, 'A' Flight, RAF Leuchars, Fife, 1955 | Having reformed in September 1951, initially on Vampire NF.10s, 151 Squadron had the distinction of being the sole night fighter defence for Scotland. Re-equipping with Meteor NF.11s during 1953, WD643 is typical of the type during this period, finished in the wartime overall Medium Sea Grey with Dark Green disruptive pattern upper surfaces to Pattern No 2. The bars flanking the fuselage roundels comprised white saltire crosses on a blue background thinly outlined with a black border. The tailplane bullet fairings were painted red or blue according to which Flight the aircraft belonged – WD643's was red, as was its aircraft letter on the fin. The Squadron badge was applied to the left side of the nose.

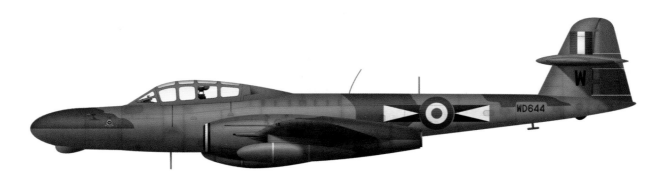

Meteor NF.11, WD644 'W', 141 Squadron, RAF Coltishall, Norfolk, 1955 | 141 Squadron became the second Night Fighter unit to re-equip with the Meteor NF.11, from September 1951, (the first being 29 Squadron). Finished in the then standard Night Fighter Scheme of overall Medium Sea Grey with Dark Green disruptive pattern upper surfaces, the black bars flanking the fuselage roundels each carried a white horizontal triangle and the engine intake lips had narrow black, white, black bands. The individual aircraft letter was carried on the fin, in black, with the Squadron badge applied to the left side of the nose.

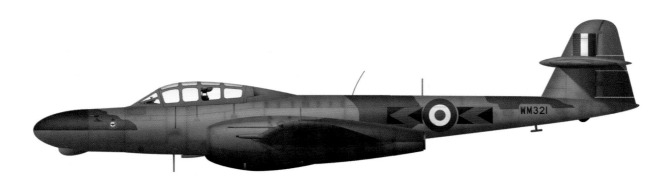

Meteor NF.13, WM321, 219 Squadron, RAF Kabrit, Egypt, 1953 | One of two Meteor NF.13-equipped squadrons in the Suez Canal Zone, (the other being 39 Squadron), 219 Squadron's jets were also finished in the wartime overall Medium Sea Grey with Dark Green disruptive pattern upper surfaces. WM321 was uncoded but carried the unit's black bars with red, forward facing, chevrons flanking the fuselage roundels and the Squadron badge on the nose. WM321 made an emergency landing on 30 April 1954 after suffering an in-flight fire and was later written-off.

Meteor NF.11 'NFII Nº 3', *Centre d'Essais en Vol*, Brétigny-sur-Orge, France, September 1980 | The *Armée de l'Air* (French Air Force) received several Meteors during the mid-late 1950s, many of which were diverted from RAF stocks. A number of Meteor NF.11s were delivered between September 1954 and April 1955 to replace the Mosquito NF.36s operated by *Escadre de Chasse* (EC) 30, until replaced in turn by the Sud Aviation *Vautour* in 1957.

Several Meteor NF.11s were subsequently transferred to the *Centre d'Essais en Vol* (CEV) in 1958, including 'Nº 3', where they were used as equipment testbeds and chase planes in a wide variety of experiments, including radar and missile tests and even toward the development of Concorde. They were later joined by two NF.13s and two ex-RAF NF.14s.

'Nº 3', illustrated here, had originally been assigned the RAF serial WM298 but was delivered directly to France instead. By September 1980, and still very much in service, it was finished in an overall light grey scheme with dark green engine nacelles. The leading edges of the wings, engine nacelle fronts, tailplane and fin were black, with a matt black anti-glare panel in front of the windscreen which contrasted with the semi-gloss nose section. French tricolour roundels were carried in all six positions and the code 'NFII Nº 3' was carried on the rear fuselage in black. Day-glo orange panels were applied to the nose, mid-fuselage, wing tips and tailplane tips, and photo calibration markings comprising a black disc with a red square in the centre on the fuselage sides, overlapping part of the roundel, and on the fuselage spine.

Currently this aircraft is on display at the Royal Museum of the Armed Forces and Military History in Brussels, Belgium.

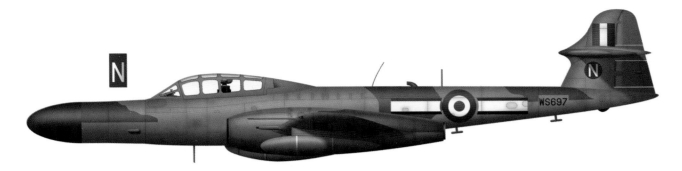

Meteor NF.12, WS697 'N', 25 Squadron, RAF West Malling, Kent, summer 1954 | 25 Squadron was re-equipped with Meteor NF.12s in March 1954 supplemented by NF.14s the following month. Still finished in the old wartime Night Fighter Scheme of overall Medium Sea Grey with Dark Green disruptive pattern upper surfaces, but with a black nose radome, WS697 is illustrated carrying the initial style of Squadron colours flanking the fuselage roundel – long silver bars with just narrow black borders at top and the bottom (these altered slightly c 1956 when the silver bars were completely outlined in black.) The white aircraft letter on the fin is on a blue (B Flight colour) disc as is the matching bullet fairing tip. At this time the engine intakes also had thin black lips. WS697 served with the unit until June 1958.

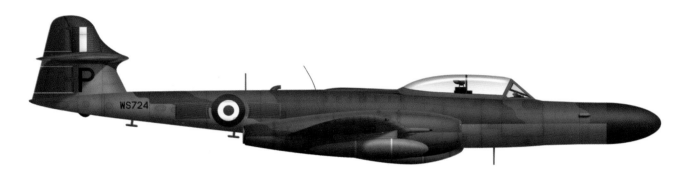

Meteor NF.14, WS724 'P', 72 Squadron, RAF Church Fenton, North Yorkshire, summer 1956 | 72 Squadron was the first Meteor F.8 day fighter squadron to change over to the night fighter role and began re-equipping with NF.12s and 14s in February 1956. Starting with the NF.14 production run, a new Night Fighter Scheme was introduced, comprising Dark Sea Grey and Dark Green upper surfaces with Light Aircraft Grey undersides, the demarcation between the upper and under surfaces on the fuselage sides, initially being the same mid-point level (similar to Pattern No.2) as the previous Medium Sea Grey and Dark Green scheme. WS724 was finished in this new scheme in which, it should be noted, the lower fin was in the under surface colour, whereas the fin's upper section was in the upper surface colours.

Meteor NF.14, WS800 'A', 60 Squadron, RAF Tengah, Singapore, early 1960 | Refurbished and 'tropicalised' with cockpit cooling intakes fitted (as per NF.13s), Meteor NF.14s were sent to 60 Squadron at Tengah in late 1959 to replace the unit's existing Venom FB.4s. WS800 was finished in the new Night Fighter Scheme of Dark Sea Grey and Dark Green upper surfaces with a low fuselage demarcation line which, apparently, was applied to most if not all of the NF.14s allocated to the Far East. The under surfaces are thought to be Light Aircraft Grey, but some NF.14s may have had HSS undersides. Another feature of the NF.14's modified scheme was that the fin and rudder below the level of the tailplane was now finished in upper surface Dark Sea Grey/Dark Green and the fuselage serial numbers were applied in white. 60 Squadron's fuselage bars were also revised prior to journeying to Singapore – the white flashes on the black fuselage bars were stylistically different from those carried by the 'old' NF.12/NF.14s used by 60 Squadron crews prior to leaving for the Far East in their 'new' NF.14s. WS800 was adopted by the CO, Sqn Ldr Rex Knight, and coded 'A' outlined in black (on the nosewheel door). It carried broad black, and narrow white, horizontal stripes across the lower section of the fin and rudder over which the blue head of a markhor (antelope) was applied. The Squadron badge, and a Squadron Leader's pennant (above which were the names in small white lettering of the Squadron Leader and his senior navigator), were carried on the port side of the nose.

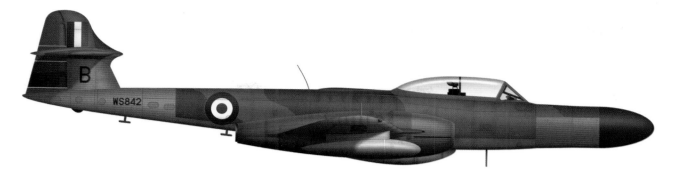

Meteor NF(T).14, WS842 'B', 2 Air Navigation School, RAF Thorney Island, West Sussex, mid-1960 | 2 ANS operated a variety of aircraft types which, by the late-1950s, included ten modified Meteor NF.14s. At least fourteen redundant airframes were adapted to become NF(T).14s to provide further training for navigators destined for fast jet operations. All NF(T).14s were transferred to 1 ANS at Stradishall in early 1962 and used until replaced by Dominies c February 1966. Originally finished in the modified Dark Sea Grey/Dark Green upper surface scheme with low fuselage demarcation and Light Aircraft Grey under surfaces (applied to operational Night Fighters at the time), ample quantities of day-glo orange was then applied for service with 2 ANS. The aircraft code 'B' was black, as was the fuselage serial and nose radome. Later, while serving with 1 ANS, WS842's camouflage was removed and replaced by High Speed Silver overall plus abundant quantities of day-glo stripes.

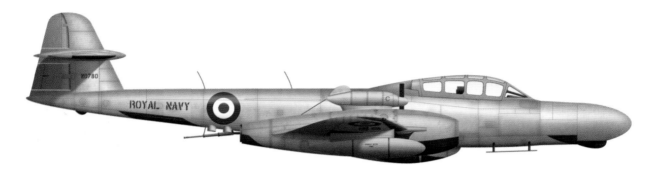

Meteor TT.20, WD780, 776 Fleet Requirements Unit, Hurn Airport, 1961 | The TT.20 was a dedicated target towing aircraft used by the Fleet Air Arm and the RAF, created by modifying surplus NF.11s and fitting them with a wind-driven ML Aviation Type G winch, mounted above the starboard wing which controlled a 6,000ft long cable, capable of towing Rushton, Sleeve and Banner targets for air-to-air and surface-to-air target practice. Finished in the overall HSS scheme, with 'bright' post-war roundels in six positions, the undersides of many of the Royal Navy's TT.20s featured the paler Saturn Yellow shade specifically chosen for RN Target Tugs, with black diagonal bands, as illustrated by WD780. Also of note are the stencil-style serial number presentation and ROYAL NAVY legend on the rear fuselage, causing the 'fuselage' serial to be re-located to the fin.

Meteor TT.20, WD630 'Q', 3/4 Civilian Anti-Aircraft Co-operation Unit, Exeter, 1964 | Like the RN, the RAF made significant use of the Meteor TT.20, primarily with Civilian Anti-Aircraft Co-operation Units whose aircraft, such as WD630 illustrated here, were flown by civilian pilots. Finished in High Speed Silver with the Target Tug Yellow and Black diagonal band under surfaces scheme, WD630 has adhesive day-glo strips applied on the rear fuselage, nose, wings and engine nacelles.

Modelling the Meteor

Many Meteor kits have been produced over the past 50 years but, for reasons already alluded too, we have purposely confined our selection to kits of significant modelling interest or that we believe may still be available at the time of publication.

MINIWING
1/144 scale

Meteor T.7 (MINI084)
The Miniwing 1/144 scale Gloster Meteor T.7 is a resin kit consisting of fourteen cream-coloured parts with a choice of a clear-resin canopy or a vacformed canopy. Also included is a set of masks for the canopy. There are decals for two overall silver RAF T.7s. Construction is simple with all major parts being single pieces, so after painting the cockpit interior and applying the seat and instrument panel decals, the cockpit can be added into the fuselage, followed by attaching the full span single-piece wing, full span single-piece horizontal tailplane and then the auxiliary fuel tank under the fuselage. After painting and decaling the model, the undercarriage legs and undercarriage doors can be added to complete the construction which will result in a good-looking 1/144 scale model of a two-seat Meteor.

Miniwings have announced a (resin) Meteor F.8 (MINI085) as a future release.

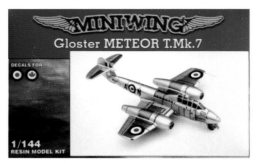

AEROCLUB
1/72 scale

Sadly no longer generally available following John Adams' decision to stop production of all his wonderful limited-run kits, the company's Meteors are still well worth a mention.

Aeroclub initially produced four injection-moulded conversions for the Matchbox 1/72 Meteor night fighter. Later, they made the F.8 and T.7 as full multi-medium (injected-moulded plastic, white metal and vacform) kits. A range of 1/48 scale kits (see 1/48 scale section) were produced, all of which were vacform-based multi-medium kits.

Meteor F.8
This kit was originally released in the 1990s and had injection-moulded main parts (e.g. fuselage, wings, tailplanes etc), with white metal parts (e.g. undercarriage and cockpit interior) and a vacformed canopy. The decal sheet featured markings for 55, 504 and 616 Squadrons RAF and 77 Squadron RAAF.

Meteor T.7
Similar to the F.8 above, this kit was also first released in the 1990s and comprised injection-moulded main parts (featuring a new twin-seater fuselage and optional tailplanes), white metal parts and a vacformed canopy. Decal sheet had markings for 502 Squadron RAF and WA669, of the CFS's Vintage Pair.

Both kits were accurate in their dimensions and shape, and went together well, with just a little added care being needed due to the nature of their being limited-production which resulted in slightly thicker plastic mouldings and lack of locating pins and holes, but they were as well moulded as most mainstream kits.

Following the release of the new-mould technology Airfix F.8 and MPM T.7, they would have been somewhat superseded had they still been available, and are perhaps now best regarded as collectors' items.

AIRFIX
1/72 scale

Meteor F.3 (A50039)
Originally released in 1970, this kit has remained in the Airfix catalogue 'on and off' throughout the company's ups and downs and changes of ownership, and is currently available at the time of writing. A product of the time, it is generally accurate but showing its age, with raised panel lines and masses of rivets. Decals were for 616 Squadron's EE239 YQ-Q, but more recently (*circa* 2015) the kit has been re-boxed with a V1 Flying Bomb and additional 74 Squadron markings. With a bit of effort, skill and ingenuity, a decent model can still be built from this kit.

Meteor F.8 (A03076)
Re-boxing of the MPM Meteor F.8 (see MPM section later)

CYBER-HOBBY

1/72 scale

Meteor F.3 (CH5044)

Released in 2010, this was a much needed 21st Century mainstream update on the venerable Airfix kit. The five grey sprues are superbly detailed with crisply engraved detailing and no rivets. The kit has a fully detailed cockpit with sidewalls that incorporate the nosewheel well. Separate rudder, ailerons, elevators and flaps are included. A small photo-etch fret provides the upper and lower air brakes that fit into their bays in the wings, but Cyber-Hobby have missed the opportunity to include seat belts on the fret. A clear, three-piece canopy is included that can be posed open or closed. The instructions provide detail shots for proper alignment, but no interior, wheel well or undercarriage leg colour information is provided. Markings are provided for eight aircraft – four 616 Sqn at Lubeck and Manston 1945, in camouflage and overall white; 74 Sqn in 1945 and 257 Sqn in 1947, both in camouflage and a High Speed Silver (HSS) finished aircraft from 500 Sqn RAuxAF in 1948. The decals are well printed, providing the Sky fuselage band and a full set of stencils.

Meteor F.1 (CH5084)

The Meteor F.1, was released in 2011 in the Golden Wing Series and is Cyber-Hobby's follow-on to their earlier Meteor F.3. Again, the kit appears to be accurate thanks to the use of the latest high-tech slide mould techniques. The surface is well detailed with engraved panel lines, and new parts to make detailed Welland jet engines, which fit in brand-new wings. To further reflect the differences between the F.3 and F.1, the kit features a new canopy with the earlier 'hinged' hood, which looks accurate. Choice of decals is less than the F.3 reflecting the F.1's limited use with just a 616 Sqn machine based at Manston in mid-1944, and EE210/G which was sent for USAAF evaluation at Muroc Air Base, (now Edwards AFB) in southern California, February 1944.

FROG

1/72 scale

Meteor F.4

Like the Airfix F.3, Frog's F.4 was originally released in 1970, and features similar basic detail and raised panel lines – but no rivets. Generally accurate, the nose might be just a bit too bulbous and the wing trailing edges are overly thick, but it was a nice simple build. Following the demise of Frog in 1977, the kit has been marketed by several east European companies and may still be selectively available. However, the kit has been overtaken by other manufacturers' offerings such as MPM's F.4. The original Frog decals were for two silver aircraft one from 263 Sqn RAF and the other from 323 Sqn Royal Netherlands Air Force.

Frog produced a 1/72 scale Meteor F.8 in the late 1950s which is now a collectors' item.

CZECH MASTER RESIN

1/72 scale

Meteor F.8/FR.9

When released in 1999, a good kit of the Meteor F.8 was long overdue. Being resin it may not have received the exposure it deserved, but at the time it was most definitely the best 1/72 Meteor F.8 out there. Moulded in resin throughout, with a vac-formed canopy, the surface detail is finely recessed and easily rivalled that of current injection moulded kits.

The breakdown of parts makes assembly easy – the wing is a solid piece, with the lower halves of the engine nacelles moulded with it. The upper nacelles are separate with inserts for the tailpipes and the wing leading edges of the wing that are visible from the front of the nacelle. The fuselage is moulded in two halves with the fin, and the cockpit comprises a floor, instrument panel, seat, rudder pedals, and control column, with sidewall detail moulded on the fuselage sides.

Careful weighting will be needed to avoid a tail-sitter, luckily the separate noses are hollow, giving room to add weight, with additional weight being added in the fuselage underneath the cockpit – making it a very heavy model. It's a good job the landing gear is robust! The gear doors are thinly moulded with interior detailing.

Options available include: two sets of engine intakes; two noses for the F.8 and FR.9 (the latter's nose has open camera ports, but no 'glass', it is left to the modeller to prepare windows from leftover plastic from the vacformed canopies); two choices of canopies with a spare for each; a full set of stores including rockets, bombs, and fuel tanks. The decal choices offer markings for six Meteors – from Australia, Israel, and the RAF, the most colourful being an F.8 from 66 Sqn with blue and white striped tailplanes and matching Squadron bars, and IDF/AF machines wearing yellow/black Suez Crisis stripes.

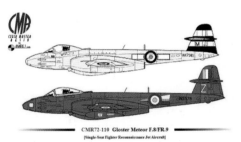

CMR72-110 Gloster Meteor F.8/FR.9
[Single-Seat Fighter Reconnaissance Jet Aircraft]

MPM

1/72 scale

MPM's Meteor family were initially developed in conjunction with Hannants to provide those variants not already kitted by the mainstream manufacturers such as Airfix, Frog and Matchbox, hence the close Xtrakit connection. Despite being short-run products, they have similar engineering and production standards to those of the mainstream manufacturers'. The kits are all packaged in sturdy boxes with attractive box art, and the part sprues, transparencies and decals are all individually bagged. All the kits contain over 75 parts (on two main sprues) moulded in a mid-grey plastic that is easy to work with, although as with any kit of this kind, careful trimming and sanding of the mating surfaces is needed and they require careful alignment.

Regardless of the Mark, generally all the kits offer one sprue frame of common parts that forms the basis of the wing, nacelles, undercarriage that are common to all the variants. The detail is good including wheel wells and multi-piece undercarriage. The wings are moulded in six parts with top and bottom halves for the centre section and separate wing panels outboard of the engines, which is where the only real criticism for these kits lie, as the outer wing panels are simply butt joined to the wing centre section and it is left to the modeller to ensure the correct 6° of dihedral. This part's frame also includes the narrow and enlarged engine intakes that are applicable to some late versions. The undercarriage assembly is another of the minor weaknesses of MPM's short-run tooling. Not only are there vague and shallow attachment points for the legs where they meet the roof of their respective wheel bays, but each leg consists of (too?) many parts – at least for anyone with less than perfect eyesight – with too many joins needing to be critically aligned and the requirement of scrap plastic/stretched sprue mudguard stays.

The second sprue frame provides the specific Mark/sub-type parts, such as the fuselage halves, tailplanes, cockpit detail with seat(s), control column(s), side consoles and instrument panel(s). No sidewall details are included although the above is adequate for

displaying a model with the canopy closed. This sprue also provides the optional wing or ventral fuel tanks. At least 10 grams of noseweight is required – tucked in the nose, and around and under the cockpit.

The transparencies, moulded as single pieces, are generally clear, thin and free of distortion, but are quite brittle and need to be carefully separated from the sprue. Gun sights are included as clear parts. There are essentially eight kits available...

Meteor F.1 (MPM72567)
This kit is basically an F.3 (the wing has 'Meteor Mk.III 1/72' moulded on it) with F.4 fuselage sprues, and an F.1 canopy and decals. The ailerons are the same as the F.3's – which is incorrect as the F.1's ailerons sported a horn-balance and a differently located trim-tab. No resin or photo-etch is included.

Meteor F.4 (MPM72554)
Released around 2013, the MPM Meteor F.4 is perhaps the least kitted Mark of this classic first generation British jet and therefore all the more welcome following the demise of the of the 1970s vintage Frog kit. There are few problems in its construction with perhaps the exception of joining and setting the dihedral of the outer wing panels as mentioned above. The wing sprue is also used for the F.8 version with the larger intake openings (not used on the F.4) included. The F.4s come in at least two box-top offerings – *Fuerza Aérea Argentina* and Belgian AF – with the appropriate selection of decal options.

Meteor T.7 (MPM72548)
A new two-seater trainer fuselage with a clear, long-framed canopy, together with (essentially) standard F.4/F.8 plastic parts – plus, in the 'Commonwealth Trainer' Hi-tech boxing, a substantial bag of resin offering a full interior to both cockpits including a full floor and nosewheel bay roof, bucket seats and full side wall and instrument panel detail which also has a separate etched fret for both flight instrument panels and film instruments and a vinyl canopy mask. Other useful options include early and late style intakes and drop tanks. Decal markings are for five T.7s including WS103 'VL' of 709 NAS, RNAS Yeovilton, 1960; WH144 'N-A' of 215 AFS RAF, 1953; and three 77 Sqn RAAF, T.7s circa 1950.

Meteor F.8 Hi-Tech (MPM72531)
These kits contain the usual two sprues of plastic parts and a clear injected-moulded canopy, plus additional resin (although much of the resin could have been produced in plastic in the first place), and photo-etch parts, with an extended ten-page instruction booklet and decals for three aircraft. There is no indication as to how much noseweight is required or even that it is needed, but be assured, it is! The large belly tank, and two wing tanks are included.

Meteor F.8 (MPM72543) with 77 Sqn RAAF decals
The same as the Hi-Tech F.8 above but without the extra resin and photo-etch parts. The decal sheet offers five RAAF machines and is also marketed by Xtrakit.

Meteor FR.9 (MPM72534)

The FR.9 is essentially the same kit as the F.8 with two grey sprues and one clear, with a new clear FR.9 nose in two halves. This means that the integrally moulded F.8 nose already on the fuselage needs to be cut off and replaced with the new one. Three markings options are provided – two from 208 Sqn (one in HSS and the other in camouflage

with large patches of orange on the tip of the engine nacelles, and black and yellow 'Suez Stripes' for Operation *Musketeer* in 1956). The third is a camouflaged aircraft from 8 Sqn. Decals are well printed but some parts of the various options will have to be hand painted to match the stripes given.

Meteor PR.10 (MPM72560)

The PR.10 is essentially the same kit as the F.8 with the wings and tailplanes of the F.4 added into the box and new bits including the clear FR.9/(PR.10) photo nose and a pair of resin rear wing root extensions. Again, it is left to the modeller to cut away the nose, and the tail section, of the F.8 fuselage and replace them with the photo nose and F.4 rear fuselage, fin and rudder parts provided for which the new tail has a circular tab that will help in alignment. The outer wing sections are still butt-joined and the same applies with the new nose. No cameras are provided and there is no indication of where the fuselage cameras might have been placed. There are five decal options – two from 541 Sqn; one in Dark Green/Medium Sea Grey over PRU Blue, the other in the Medium Sea Grey over PRU Blue; a 13 Sqn machine in overall HSS based in Egypt during 1953; and an 81 Sqn machine, the personal mount of the CO, in HSS, Singapore in 1960.

Trent Meteor 'First Turboprop Fighter' (MPM72574)

MPM's Meteor F.1 mouldings, the kit contains three sprues of grey plastic parts with engraved panel lines, an injected moulded canopy and an additional bag of resin parts for a pair of RR RB.50 Trent turbo-prop engine cowlings and five-blade propellers plus auxiliary tailplane finlets to help with directional stability. The modeller is required to do all the modification surgery (on the basic F.1 mouldings) and as such, this is a kit best suited to advanced modellers. Decals are included for EE227/G.

Meteor F.8 (PRONE) (MPM72569)

MPM's standard Meteor F.8 kit with an additional sprue tree with injection-moulded grey plastic prone nose halves and interior parts, rear fuselage, and fin halves with leading edge fillets. The modeller is required to remove the F.8's nose and add the prone section. There is an additional clear sprue tree with a Prone Pilot nose canopy, plus decals for WK935.

PJ PRODUCTIONS   1/72 scale

Meteor F.4, (721004), T.7 (721009 & 72-1010), F.8 (72-1002), NF.11 (72-1012)

These are full resin kits, which include vacform and photo-etch parts and decals. Being all resin they are quite heavy especially as everything in front of their centre-of-gravity is solid resin to avoid tail sitting. Quality of the resin casting is excellent with only a few air

bubbles needing to be filled. A problem associated with these kits is the shape of the wing tips, which do not appear square enough. Parts breakdown is quite simple, with separate noses and tails to accommodate different variants. As PJ Productions is a Belgian manufacturer most of the decal choices, represent Belgian Air Force machines.

REVELL

1/72 scale

Meteor F.4 (04658)

This is a re-boxing of the MPM F.4 kit released in 2011 – but at roughly half the price of the MPM boxing here in the UK. The surface detail has finely engraved panel lines, but unlike most other Revell kits there are no location pins/holes on the major parts, so extra care will be needed during construction. The parts come on two flash-free sprues while the canopy, which is clear but a little thick, is in a separate bag. Instructions have been re-drawn by Revell and they recommend 10 grams of weight in the nose, which will be needed given the extent of the airframe aft of the mainwheels. Decals are for two RAF aircraft – a 1 Sqn

machine based at RAF Tangmere in 1950 with the striking red markings as featured on the box art, and a 600 Sqn RAuxAF machine based at RAF Biggin Hill 1951.

SPECIAL HOBBY

1/72 scale

Meteor F.4 'World Speed Record' (SH72361)

Special Hobby is a Czech-based kit manufacturer and part of the MPM consortium, and this is the standard MPM F.4 kit re-boxed and marketed by Special Hobby. The kit contains markings for EE455, one of two Meteor F.3s built to F.4 standard and used by the RAF High Speed Flight in the World Speed Record attempt in November 1945.

Meteor T.7 (SH72548)

The standard basic MPM kit marketed under the Special Hobby label.

Meteor T.7½ (SH72317)

This kit is a standard MPM T.7 kit with an additional sprue containing an MPM F.8 rear fuselage and fin/rudder halves and tailplanes, to allow the handful of Meteor T.7s fitted with the F.8 fin to be modelled. Such hybrids were colloquially termed Meteor T.7½.

XTRAKIT

1/72 scale

Meteor F.8 (XK72001)

Xtrakit's debut release was the MPM Meteor F.8 mouldings re-boxed under Hannant's Xtrakit label. It includes early and late style

canopies and large and small engine intakes. Decals are included for three aircraft, VZ495 'ZD-K' of 222 Sqn, WH470 600 Sqn RAuxAF, both in overall HSS with early canopies and VZ494 of 501 Sqn RAuxAF, in camouflage with the late style canopy. Markings for seventeen other RAF squadrons can be found on Xtradecal X72057 and a further twelve on Xtradecal X72114 and X72115.

Meteor NF.11/12/13/14 (XK72002)

The second full kit from Xtrakit is actually the old Matchbox Meteor NF.11/12/14 kit (now owned by Revell), re-boxed with new decals. A few words about the Matchbox Meteor NF.11/12/14 may be appropriate here. It was one of Matchbox's later offerings and does not suffer from the deep panel lines associated with that company's earlier kits. In fact, this one has raised panel lines for all except flight control surfaces. Unlike the initial Matchbox releases, it is also moulded in one colour, a light grey.

Despite its age the kit is remarkably crisp and clean with only a small amount of flash on a few parts. The cockpit is basic and generic with seats, floor, instrument panels and control column for the pilot. There are options to make one of four variants – due to separate fins, large and small engine intakes, cockpit areas, canopy sections and windscreens (which are a bit thick but relatively clear). There are two noses (one for the NF.11/13 and a longer one for the NF.12/14) for which there is plenty of room in both for nose weight.

Three markings options are provided – a French NF.11 from ECN 1/30 in the 1950s, a 64 Sqn RAF NF.12, and a NF.14 also from 64 Sqn. Decals are well done and include stencils.

Meteor T.7 (XK72005)
Another re-boxing of an MPM kit by Hannants, containing seventy-seven grey plastic parts, two clear canopies, a canopy paint mask and markings for two aircraft – WF722 'Y' Target Towing Flight, RAF Akrotiri, and WL380 74 Sqn RAF Horsham St. Faith, 1958. Featuring crisply engraved panel lines and a good level of detail including drop tanks. The only disadvantage with these MPM/Xtrakit kits is that there are no locating/alignment pins for the major parts so some modelling experience will be helpful.

AIRFIX

1/48 scale

Meteor F.8 (A09182 and A09184)
At the time of writing, this offering from Airfix is the most recent mainstream Meteor F.8 kit in 1/48 scale, produced with the latest CAD design technology. The plastic is the same as this manufacturer's other recent releases – with excellent surface texture and fine, crisply engraved panel lines, fine raised rivets and raised panels where appropriate. There are 156 parts in light blue/grey plastic and eleven in clear. However, as with all these new CAD-designed Airfix kits, the tolerances are very tight, and care will be needed in assembly.

The general shape and dimensions look right. The cockpit interior is well detailed, with side panel inserts and an instrument panel with raised dial and switch detail for which the instrument dial decals provided should work well over. Most of the details are integrally-moulded, which, when the interior is painted black and some subtle dry brushing applied, is more than acceptable.

The Martin Baker Mk.2 ejection seat is made up of six pieces with alternative parts for the pan and backrest – one with harness straps moulded in place and one without.

The cockpit is built in conjunction with the fuselage cannon bays and the forward undercarriage bay. The four 20mm cannon are included as separate items and include the magazines, and as the gun bay doors are separate you can display them if desired. Nose weight isn't included and this kit is going to need plenty to stop it tail-sitting – but the problem is, with all the interior detail included, where to put it! Tamiya (see later) included a shaped metal weight in their kit (which helped to solve the problem although even more weight is ideally required), and it's a shame that Airfix haven't followed their lead.

The clear sprue contains a separate windscreen and two separate canopy hoods – the early-style hood with the covered rear fairing and the later all-clear style – a landing light, and what appear to be the nose camera windows for an FR.9 or PR.10 – indicating future releases? Wing tip navigation lights are moulded solid with the wings.

The wings have separate upper halves, which attach to a one-piece full span lower wing section. The undercarriage bay front and rear walls and the engine mounts are moulded as part of main wing spars over which the main undercarriage sidewalls slot making for a rigid fit. Two detailed Rolls-

Royce Derwent 8 engines are included, with full length exhaust tubes and the choice is offered to display them in situ in the engine bays or to display one on a trolley, supplied in the kit, or just have them sealed up with the separate top engine covers fitted.

All the undercarriage legs are well detailed, and as the fuselage nose cone is separate, it allows the nosewheel retraction mechanism assembly (attached to the front of the cockpit tub), to be added later. The wheels are supplied with and without flats on the tyres, and there are optional undercarriage doors, fitted from the inside of the wing, for those wanting to build their Meteor with a retracted undercarriage. The rudder, elevator and ailerons are all separate parts and can be posed to taste. Speed brakes are separate too, and may be glued open or closed.

Both the small and large diameter engine intakes are provided plus a pair of underwing tanks and the conformal ventral tank. Boarding step and the shell ejection chutes are supplied separately. There are no rockets or

launch rails, but flashed over holes for these are on the inside of the lower wing halves presumably for the RAAF boxing (A09184).

The 16-page A4 instruction booklet is clear and features illustrated steps, with an A3 foldout sheet for the full colour painting/decal guide for both version supplied. Decals are included for two Meteor F.8s – WL123 of 111 Squadron, RAF North Weald, Essex, 1954, and WH364 of 85 Squadron, RAF Binbrook, Lincolnshire, 1968. Full stencil data is included and a clear diagram showing where each tiny item goes.

AEROCLUB

1/48 scale

During the 1990s, Aeroclub released a multi-medium 1/48 scale Meteor F.8. Packed in a stout box, the kit comprised two thick white vacform sheets containing the fuselage halves, wings, jet nozzles, nacelle blanking plates, optional wing tanks and ventral fuel tank. Surface detail was a little soft and heavy but looked okay under a coat of paint.

The cockpit tub, tailplanes and main gear doors were supplied in caramel-coloured, low-pressure, short run injection-moulded plastic, with the undercarriage gear, nosewheel doors and other small details in white metal. The forward nacelles were cast in resin. Markings were provided for two RAF and one RAAF aircraft. The instructions were quite good, with a written narrative, scale plans and two exploded views to assist assembly.

The F.8 was followed some time later by an NF.14, again primarily a vacform, with a resin cockpit tub, radar instrument panel and forward intake sections of the engine nacelles with injection-moulded tail surfaces. White metal parts were provided for the landing gear, seats, and other small detail parts. It is interesting to record that it was in this kit's instructions that note was first made of the fact that almost all previous research on the NF.14 had incorrectly identified the Mark as having a longer fuselage extension than the other night fighters.

Decals were provided for a 46 Sqn machine in the Dark Sea Grey and Dark Green upper surfaces with Light Aircraft Grey under surfaces in 1955, and a 60 Sqn aircraft in 1960 with similar upper surface camouflage and aluminium lower surfaces. Neither the F.8 nor the NF.14 are in production or available.

CLASSIC AIRFRAMES

1/48 scale

In the early-to-mid-2000s, Classic Airframes released a series of 1/48 scale Meteor kits, which are long out of production but still worthy of mention.

Primarily comprising short-run injection-moulded plastic, with resin parts for the cockpit, engines and undercarriage, the kits were typical of Classic Airframes at the time,

essentially accurate but with some construction challenges, especially around the fit of the intake parts.

However, with patience and time, excellent result could be achieved, and examples my still be found for sale at model shows and on e-bay.

Meteors F.4, F.8 (early), F.8 (late), FR.9, T.7 and NF.11/13

TAMIYA   1/48 scale

Meteor F.1 (61051 initial release) and Meteor F.1 (61065 updated re-release)

Initially released in 1997, Tamiya's 'Meteor Mk.I' was accidentally tooled using the Gloster F.9/40, DG202, which combined an F.1 fuselage with an F.3 wing. Apparently DG202 had once suffered an engine fire which destroyed the wing and so an F.3 wing was fitted as a replacement; thus, strictly speaking, the kit was accurate – but only for airframe at the museum! The main problem was the inclusion of airbrakes in the wings, which were fitted to F.3s, and the associated truncated undercarriage fairing blisters. To their credit, Tamiya re-tooled the wing and got it right for a standard production F.1, and re-released the kit in 1999. Unfortunately, they did not change the box art, and for some time, modellers were left wondering which version of the kit was in the shrink-wrapped box they were buying!

Typically Tamiya, the kit is well engineered, combining simple stress-free assembly with overall good fit. Surface detail is excellent with finely engraved panel lines and delicately raised details. A cylindrical nose weight, which fits immediately behind the cockpit tub is supplied although it is only just sufficient to keep the nose down – ideally a just a bit more weight is needed.

Assembly is straightforward and no filler is needed. The fit of the separate wing root fairings needs care and the nacelle fronts/wing leading edge sections will benefit from some gentle sanding to achieve a perfect fit as do the separate detachable tops of the nacelles, in a choice of either opaque or clear plastic. The main undercarriage legs are simple and nicely detailed and lock positively into place to ensure perfect alignment. The nosewheel assembly is also simple but sturdy enough to cope with the nose weight. The main undercarriage bays are moulded in with the top wing halves, and are a little under-detailed and the cannon ports could do with drilling out and sections of metal tubing inserting to simulate the cannon barrels.

Two reasonably detailed Rolls-Royce W.2B/23 Welland I engines are included, that can be displayed in situ in the engine bays, visible either by leaving off the detachable separate tops of the nacelles or fitting the clear plastic equivalents. None of the control surfaces are separate.

A full, eight part, Fieseler Fi 103/V-1 'Flying Bomb' is included in the box, together with a nine-part trolley.

Decals are provided for three F.1s of 616 Sqn in 1944 – EE216 'YQ-E', EE219 'YQ-D' and 'YQ-G'. They are typically thick Tamiya decals that settle down well under a coat or two of Micro-Set/Sol. The markings provide squadron codes Sky tail band, as well as the yellow wing leading edges.

Meteor F.3 (61083)

Presumably using the original/initial wing tooling from the 'accidental' F.1 kit, Tamiya released an F.3 variant in 2002, correctly featuring the wing-mounted airbrakes, and including a different front windscreen coaming and rear decking section for the F.3's three-piece sliding 'blown' canopy hood. Otherwise, Tamiya's F.3 is essentially the same mouldings as the F.1, for which the above comments apply.

Shorter jet pipes and the small nacelle-mounted intakes for the Derwent I powered

F.3s (although the first fifteen F.3s were still Welland-powered), are included (parts C10 x2 and C11 x2) but both the decal choices, EE235 'YQ-H', and EE239 'YQ-Q' – finished in the overall white scheme – provided in this particular boxing were Welland-engined.

Subsequent releases of this kit may involve instructions and decals for Derwent-engined F.3s.

HONG KONG MODELS

1/32 scale

Meteor F.4 (HKM01E05)

The parts are on three large medium grey sprues, with engraved panel lines and riveted areas. The fuselage is in vertically split halves, with a separate rudder, and the mainplanes in upper wing halves and a full span lower wing half. The cockpit floor is moulded integrally with the nosewheel well and there are detailed port and starboard cockpit sidewalls, a rear bulkhead, plain seat, control column, instrument panel and footboards with rudder bar. Once assembled though, the cockpit interior looks a little sparse, the throttles especially being somewhat indistinct. The prominent gunsight needs additional detailing, especially the removal of the opaque plastic gunsight glass with a clear piece, although separate cannon barrels are provided that slot in to the rear of the troughs, and some nose weight is provided.

The canopy is moulded in three clear sections, allowing the hood to be posed open, although in some boxings, it was reported that the windscreen had a slight moulding ridge, which was barely noticeable but could be seen at certain angles.

The wings have separate ailerons and the tailplane separate elevators, both with separate trim tabs. The flaps and the four airbrakes above and below the wings are also separate. No engines are provided, but engine fronts are that fit behind large splitter wedges that are a bit overscale and look more like bulkheads, although once assembled not much can be seen in there. There may also be a problem with the size of the engine intakes, which fall somewhere between the early 'nar-

row' and the later 'wide' versions, but there are aftermarket replacements available (e.g. from Fisher Models), for those who deem it necessary. The rest of the kit appears to be more or less generally accurate.

The undercarriage legs are moulded in halves, and include integrally moulded mudguards and retraction arms but are suitably detailed. The wheels, (nose and main), are also moulded in halves together with the hubs, which might have been better as separate parts in this scale. The ventral fuel tank is also included.

The instruction booklet is well printed, and the decal sheet provides markings for two F.4s – RA381 of 600 'City of London' Sqn with wartime and post-war style roundels in the dull and bright colours, and C-027 (ex-EE527) of the *Fuerza Aérea Argentina*.

Despite the kit's scale, there aren't that many parts, especially considering the retail price, and it's almost as if HK Models have rushed this kit into production before all the finer details had been produced. In some of the first release boxings a four-part 1/144 scale 'solid' Meteor desktop model was included, although no decals were included for it.

ALLEY CAT CONVERSION SETS

While not full kits as such, Alley Cat produce a range of conversion sets for Meteor Target Drones in 1/72 and 1/48 scales. There is also a 1/32 scale U.15 conversion for the Hong Kong Model F.4 kit.

1/72 Meteor U.15 and U.16/21

These sets comprise the special wing tip parts, new nose cone, RVMDI radomes, wing pylons and targets, engine mounted flare packs, updated instrument panel, and some of the larger aerials in resin and small photo-etched sheets – the U.15 set is designed for the MPM F.4 kit, and the U.16/21 for Xtrakit/MPM/Airfx F.8 kits, but could be adapted to fit other manufacturers' kits. Decals are supplied for the various airframes.

1/48 Meteor U.15 and U.16/21

Similar sets to those in 1/72 scale these comprise special wing tip parts, new nose cone, RVMDI radomes, wing pylons and targets, engine mounted flare packs, updated instrument panel, and some of the larger aerials in resin and photo-etched sheets – U.15 set is designed for the Classic Airframes F.4 kit, and the U.16/21 set for the new Airfix 1/48 F.8. Again decals are supplied for the various airframes.

1/32 Meteor U.15

This set is made to order and purchasers are asked to allow 2-3 weeks for manufacture and supply. The set features over 20 parts, plus a decal sheet for three aircraft, from Llanbedr, the Royal Navy and Woomera, Australia.

Top left and above: Miniwing's kit of the Meteor T.7, which builds into a neat model, finished here as a Royal Navy trainer of 728 NAS as seen at Lossiemouth in the early 1950s. *Model and photos by Huw Morgan*

Top right: A collection of 'home made' resin and wood Meteor models built over a period of 40 years from a basic Meteor F.8 mould from which several alternative moulds were made with, short nacelles, two-seat cockpits, original 'long' wings etc. Models include single-seat Meteor F.1, F.3, F.4s, F.8s, FR.9s and a PR.10; twin-seater Trainer T.7s; Night Fighter NF.11s, NF.13s and NF.14s; a TT.20, and several U.15/U.16/U.21 Target Drones, and the Gloster E28/39, W4041/G. *Models and photo by Terry Patrick*

Centre and bottom Meteor F.3, EE253 'A6-E' of 257 Sqn at Church Fenton from September 1946 to April 1947. Built from the Dragon/Cyber Hobby kit using the kit decals. *Model by Francis Chapman; photos by Bill Newton*

Top left and right: Meteor F.8, WF677, served as W/C Shaw's personal aircraft when he was Wing Leader of 19, 72 and 85 Sqns at Church Fenton in October 1957. Built from the Xtrakit with markings from Freightdog decal sheet 72011. *Model by Francis Chapman; photos by Bill Newton*

Centre and above: Meteor F.8, WH480, 'M' of 41 Sqn, RAF Biggin Hill, Kent, 1952, with the striking white/red/white bars, as flown by the CO Sqn Ldr John M 'Dusty' Miller. Made from the original MPM Meteor F.8 kit. *Model and photos by Roger Lindsay*

Correcting the length of Matchbox's 1/72 scale NF Meteors

Top: 1/72 scale Matchbox AW Meteor NF.11/12/13/14 kit suitably shortened and finished as an NF.14 in 85 Sqn markings.

Inset: The correct length was measured from the rear of the kit's nose cone and a scale 17-inch section removed. If done with care, no filling (or re-painting) will be needed when replacing the nose cone.

Above and right: Meteor NF(T).14, WS802, from 2 ANS – one of a pair operated by the School in this colour scheme (the rest were camouflaged). *NF Models by Tony Wilson: Photos by Bill Newton*

Tamiya Meteor F.1, EE227, 'YQ-Y' of 616 Squadron, summer 1944.
Model and photos by Rick Greenwood

Tamiya Meteor F.1, EE227, 'YQ-Y' of 616 Squadron, summer 1944.
Model and photos by Rick Greenwood

Tamiya Meteor F.3 [61083], EE235, 'YQ-H' of 616 Squadron. May 1945, as flown by W/C Warren Schrader. *Model by Francis Chapman, photos by Bill Newton*

Airfix 1/48 scale Meteor F.8, finished in Xtradecal markings used to portray VZ494 of 501 Sqn in February 1957. One of two Meteor F.8s used by 501 Sqn – a Vampire unit. *Model and photos by Rick Greenwood*

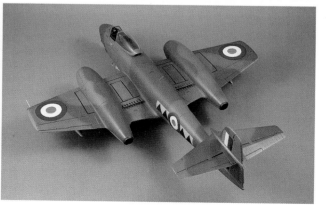

Prone Pilot Position Meteor, WK935, made from the 1/48 scale Brigade Models resin conversion kit and the 'new' Airfix Meteor F.8. *Model and photos by Bill Newton*

Airfix 1/48 scale Meteor F.8, built straight from the box, with a bit of extra detail in the cockpit and ejection seat straps added, in the markings of WH263 'N' from 616 Sqn, RAF Finningley, mid-1950s. *Model and photos by Bill Newton*

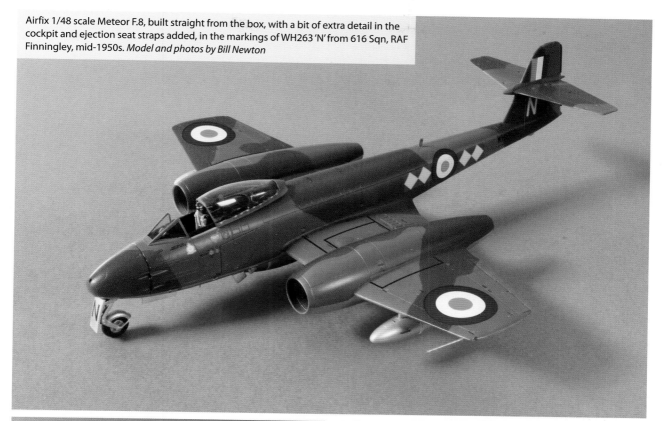

Appendices

■ APPENDIX 1   METEOR DAY FIGHTER SQUADRONS

NOTES

1) 'Period used' is the period during which listed Marks are understood to be have been on squadron strength and thus formed the operational core of the unit. However, periods of transition, as one type was replaced by another, are unavoidably included.

2) Although not specifically mentioned in Appendices 1, 2 or 3, virtually every squadron listed possessed one or more Meteor T.7s for training, hack and target towing duties and were often retained after a squadron had transitioned from the Meteor fighter to more modern designs. Similarly (and distinct from their use by numerous second-line units), single-seat Meteors were sometimes attached to operational squadrons for subsidiary purposes.

3) Unit codes are shown where applicable. In June 1950, the Air Ministry allowed fighter squadrons to replace their codes with 'fighter bars' – by which time some had already done so while others retained codes into 1951.

Squadron	Mark(s)	Period used	Comments
1 Squadron	F.3	10.46 – 8.47	Between the departure of the F.3 and arrival of the F.4 this unit employed Harvard and Oxford trainers
	F.4	5.48 – 9.50	
Code used: JX	F.8	8.50 – 9.55	
19 Squadron	F.4	1.51 – 6.51	F.4s served as interim type to assist unit conversion from DH Hornet to Meteor F.8
	F.8	4.51 – 1.57	
34 Squadron	F.8	8.54 – 11.55	The RAF's last new F.8 day fighter squadron to be formed
41 Squadron	F.4	1.51 – 5.51	As with 19 Sqn, F.4s served as interim type to assist unit conversion from DH Hornet to Meteor F.8
	F.8	4.51 – 8.55	
43 Squadron	F.4	2.49 – 9.50	Previously 266 Sqn until 11.2.49
Code: SW	F.8	9.50 – 9.54	
45 Squadron	F.8	5.55 – 29.8.55	Briefly used six Meteor F.8s (plus Vampire FB.9s) when DH Hornets were grounded in 5.55.
54 Squadron	F.8	4.52 – 3.55	Sqn re-equipped following decision to base UK air defence on the Meteor F.8.
56 Squadron	F.3	4.46 – 9.48	Swift F.1s arrived 2.54 and F.2s in 8.54. The type proved unsuccessful and was withdrawn in 3.55. Meteor F.8s retained until replaced by Hunters
	F.4	6.48 – 12.50	
Codes: ON, US	F.8	11.50 – 6.55	
63 Squadron	F.3	4.48 – 9.48	F.3s replaced Spitfire LF.16es from 4.48
	F.4	7.48 – 1.51	
Code: UB	F.8	11.50 – 1.57	
64 Squadron	F.4	1.51 – 6.51	F.4s used to aid conversion from Hornets to F.8. 64 Sqn later became NF unit with NF.12 + NF.14
(See NF appendix)	F.8	4.51 – 9.56	
65 Squadron	F.4	1.51 – 3(?).51	Replaced by Hunter F.6. conversion complete by 3.57
	F.8	2.51 – 3.57	
66 Squadron	F.3	3.47 – 5.48	F.8s replaced by 20+ Sabre F.4s, in turn replaced by 8 x Hunter F.4s in 3.56. (4 x Meteor F.8s rec'd 1956 to sustain pilot hours. With 16 Hunter F.6s on strength by 10.56 the F.8s were finally withdrawn). Code HI used into 1949
	F.4	5.48 – 1.51	
	F.8	1.51 – 4.54	
Codes: HI, LZ		(+ 1956)	
72 Squadron (See NF appendix)	F.8	7.52 – 2.56	Sqn re-equipped following decision to base UK air defence on the Meteor F.8. Converted to NF role with NF.12 + NF.14
74 Squadron	F.3	5.45 – 3.48	
	F.4	12.47 – 10.50	
Code: 4D	F.8	9.50 – 3.57	
91 Squadron	F.3	10.46 – 1.47	Became 92 Sqn 1.47
Code: DL			
92 Squadron	F.3	1.47 – 5.48	
	F.4	5.48 – 11.50	
Code: DL	F.8	10.50 – 2.54	

Squadron	Mark	Dates	Notes
111 Squadron	F.8	12.53 – 6.55	
124 Squadron Code: ON	F.3	8.45 – 4.46	Became 56 Sqn 4.46
222 Squadron Code: ZD	F.3 F.4 F.8	10.45 – 7.48 12.47 – 10.50 9.50 – 1.55	First Hunter F.1 arrived 7.12.54
234 Squadron Code: FX	F.3	2.46 – 9.46	Became 266 Sqn 1.9.46
245 Squadron Code: MR	F.3 F.4 F.8	8.45 – 4.48 12.47 – 8.50 (also 2.51 to 8.51) 6.50 – 6.57	Most F.8s were required for IFR trials following extensive mods, hence the unit rec'd 7 x F.4s for pilot currency in 1951. A few Hunter F.4s rec'd from 3.57, but Sqn DB 30.6.57
247 Squadron	F.8	4.52 – 6.55	Sqn relinquished Vampires following decision to base UK air defence on the Meteor F.8.
257 Squadron Code: A6	F.3 F.4 F.8	9.46 – 3.48 1.48 – 10.50 9.50 – 3.55	
263 Squadron Code: HE	F.3 F.4 F.8	8.45 – 3.48 12.47 – 2.51 10.50 – 7.55	Reformed 30.8.46 by renumbering 616 Squadron
266 Squadron Code: FX	F.3 F.4	9.46 – 4.48 2.48 – 2.49	Became 43 Sqn 11.2.49
500 Squadron Codes: RAA, S7	F.3 F.4 F.8	7.48 – 10.51 7.51 – 2.52 11.51 – 2.57	Sqn disbanded 10.3.57
501 Squadron	F.8		One or two sources state incorrectly that 501 Sqn (Vampires) used F.8s *operationally*. Two F.8s were rec'd in 1955 and 1956 as support aircraft – a possible source of confusion!
504 Squadron (i) Code: TM	F.3	4.45 – 8.45	Became 245 Sqn in 8.45
504 Squadron (ii) Codes: RAD, TM	F.4 F.8	10.49 – 3.52 3.52 – 2.57	Reformed 5.46. Mosquito NF.30s (5.47 – 5-48). Spit F.22s (5.48 – 2.50). Unit disbanded 10.3.57
541 Squadron Code: WY (?)	F.3	10.45 – 4.46	Disbanded 10.46. Reformed 11.47 on Spitfire PR.19s. (see Meteor Reconnaissance Squadrons)
600 Squadron Code: L J	F.4 F.8	3.50 – 4.52 11.51 – 2.57	Sqn disbanded 10.3.57
601 Squadron	F.8	8.52 – 2.57	Sqn disbanded 10.3.57
604 Squadron	F.8	8.52 – 2.57	Sqn disbanded 10.3.57
609 Squadron Code: PR	F.4 F.8	1.51 – 8.51 6.51 – 2.57	Sqn disbanded 10.3.57
610 Squadron	F.4 F.8	7.51 – 5.52 3.52 – 2.57	Sqn disbanded 10.3.57
611 Squadron	F.4 F.8	5.51 – 4.52 3.52 – 2.57	Sqn disbanded 10.3.57
615 Squadron Code: V6	F.4 F.8	9.50 – 9.51 9.51 – 2.57	Sqn disbanded 10.3.57
616 Squadron (i) Code: YQ	F.1 F.3	7.44 – 1.45 1.45 – 8.45	The only squadron to use the F.1 operationally. 616 disbanded on 30.8.45 becoming 263 Sqn
616 Squadron (ii) Codes: RAW, YQ	F.3 F.4 F.8	1.49 – 5.51 4.51 – 12.51 12.51 – 2.57	Reformed 1946, received Mosquito NF.30 in 9.47 (used until 5.49). Sqn disbanded 10.5.1957

■ APPENDIX 2 METEOR NIGHT FIGHTER SQUADRONS

Squadron	Mark(s)	Period used	Comments
5 Squadron	NF.11	21.1.59 – 16.8.60	Reformed 1.59 from 68 Sqn. Last operational user of NF.11. Javelin FAW.5s rec'd from 1.60
11 Squadron	NF.11	21.1.59 – 3.60	Reformed 1.59 from 256 Sqn. Javelin FAW.4s rec'd from 10.59
25 Squadron	NF.12 NF.14	3.54 – 7.58 1.4.54 – 7.58	Previously equipped with Vampire NF.10. Disbanded 1.7.58 – *see next entry*
25 Squadron	NF.12 NF.14	7.58 – 4.59 7.58 – 4.59	Reformed 1.7.58 by renumbering 153 Sqn. Javelin FAW.7s rec'd from 12.58
29 Squadron	NF.11 NF.12	8.51 – 11.57 2.58 – 7.58	First operational NF.11 squadron. Javelin FAW.6s rec'd 11.57 (to 8.61) plus 3 x Meteor NF.12s in 1958. Became the last front-line fighter squadron to retain TT Meteors, relinquishing T.7 (WF772) & F.8s (WF643 & WF654) in 11.65
33 Squadron	NF.12 NF.14	11.57 – 8.58 9.57 – 9.58	(1 x NF.12 rec'd [WS604]) Javelin FAW.7s rec'd from 4.7.58
39 Squadron	NF.13	3.53 – 6.58	Replaced Mosquito NF.36s
46 Squadron	NF.12 NF.14	8.54 – 2.56 8.54 – 2.56	Reformed 15.8.54 with 7 x NF.12 & 9 x NF.14 Javelin FAW.1s rec'd 24.2.56
60 Squadron	NF.12 NF.14	6.59 – 8.59 10.59 – 8.61	Both types used in UK for conversion training. Refurbished NF.14s issued when unit moved to Far East. (This unit made the very last operational flight by an RAF Meteor <u>fighter</u>)
64 Squadron	NF.12 NF.14	8.56 – 9.58 9.56 – 9.58	Previously F.8-equipped day fighter unit Javelin FAW.7s rec'd from 8.58
68 Squadron 2TAF code: A to 1954	NF.11	1.52 – 1.59	Reformed 1.1.52. Became 5 Sqn 21.1.59
72 Squadron	NF.12 NF.14	2.56 – 6.59 2.56 – 6.59	Previously F.8-equipped day fighter unit. Javelin FAW.4s rec'd 4.59 plus Javelin FAW.5s in 6.59
85 Squadron	NF.11 NF.12 NF.14	9.51 – 4.54 4.54 – 11.58 4.54 – 11.58	Disbanded 30.11.58. Reformed as a Javelin unit 1.12.58-3.63. *Reformed with Canberras on 1.4.63 as a fighter intercept training unit. Meteor T.7s & F.8s in use 9.64 to 7.70*
87 Squadron 2TAF code: B to 1954	NF.11	3.52 – 12.57	Javelin FAW.1s rec'd between 8.57 & 12.57
96 Squadron 2TAF code: L to 1954	NF.11	10.52 – 1.59	Javelin FAW.4s rec'd from 9.58. Sqn disbanded 21.1.59
125 Squadron	NF.11	3.55 – 2.56	Replaced by Venom NF.3s from 12.55
141 Squadron	NF.11	1.9.51 – 8.55	Second NF.11 sqn. Replaced by Venom NF.3s from 6.55
151 Squadron	NF.11	4.53 – 9.55	Replaced by Venom NF.3s from 7.55 (last NF.11s left 2.56)
152 Squadron	NF.12 NF.14	6.54 – 7.58 6.54 – 7.58	Reformed 6.54 Disbanded 31.7.58
153 Squadron	NF.12 NF.14	1.3.55 – 6.58 1.3.55 – 6.58	Reformed 28.2.55. Disbanded and became 25 Sqn 1.7.58
219 Squadron	NF.11 NF.13	10.52 – 5.53 4.53 – 1.9.54	Replaced Mosquito NF.36 Disbanded 1.9.54
256 Squadron 2TAF code: T to 1954	NF.11	11.52 – 1.59	Became 11 Sqn 21.1.59
264 Squadron	NF.11 NF.12 NF.14	11.51 – 11.54 1.57 – 8.57 10.54 – 9.57	Disbanded 26.9.57 – became 33 Sqn
527 Squadron	NF.11 NF.14	6.53 – 5.55 also 9.57 – 11.57 8.54 – 10.55	Squadron reformed from 'R' Calibration Sqn, Central Signals Establishment on 1.8.52. Meteor NFs operated alongside Mosquitos, Lincolns, Ansons and Varsity T.1s

Note: The four NF.11 squadrons marked '2TAF code:' were allocated to the RAF in Germany to provide some measure of night fighting capability. Other than occasional detachments from Fighter Command's meagre NF Mosquito resources, no such assets had been permanently allocated there since shortly after the end of WWII.

■ APPENDIX 3 METEOR RECONNAISSANCE SQUADRONS

Squadron	Mark(s)	Period used	Comments
2 Squadron 2TAF code: B to 1954	FR.9, PR.10, F.8	12.50 – 6.56 3.51 – 6.51	PR.10s went to 541 Sqn. 2 Sqn specialised in fighter-recce role. Swift FR.5s rec'd from 2.56
8 Squadron	FR.9	1.58 – 6.58	A Venom FB.4 unit. FR.9s formed 'C' Flight. (FR function conducted by Aden Protectorate FR Flight 9.58 – 3.60)
13 Squadron	PR.10	12.51 – 9.56	Mosquito PR.34s to 3.52. Canberra PR.7 rec'd 2.56
79 Squadron 2TAF code: T to 1954	FR.9 F.8	11.51 – 8.56 1955/56	Swift FR.5s rec'd by 8.56
81 Squadron	PR.10	12.53 – 7.61	PR.10s later supplemented by Canberra PR.7s
208 Squadron	FR.9 F.8 PR.10?	2.51 – 3.58 1955 – 1958 ?	Replaced Spitfire FR.18s.
541 Squadron Code: WY; 2TAF code: A to 1954	PR.10	12.50 – 9.57	Replaced Spitfire PR.19s. Sqn disbanded 7.9.57

■ APPENDIX 4 SELECT RAF METEOR TRAINING UNITS

Unit	Mark(s)	Unit existence	Comments
1335 (Meteor) Conversion Unit	F.1, F.3, F.4 (?)	8.3.45 – 15.8.46	Redesignated 226 OCU 15.8.46 Code: XL
226 OCU (i)	F.3, F.4, T.7	15.8.46 – 31.8.49	Disbanded (DB) 31.8.49 at Driffield (became 203 AFS). Codes used: KD, XL.
226 OCU (ii)	F.4, T.7, F.8 FR.9	1.9.49 – 3.6.55 6.51 – 6.55	Reformed (RF) at Stradishall. DB 3.6.55 1 Sqn code = HX: 2 Sqn code = KR 226 OCU (Recce Flight) used FR.9s 15.6.51 – 3.6.55 Recce Flight and Station Flight code = UU
228 OCU	NF.11, 12, NF.14, T.7*	1.5.47 – 15.9.61	228 Tactical Light Bomber & Night Fighter OCU. NF Meteors in use 1952-1961 (Javelins rec'd from1957)
229 OCU	T.7 F.8*	15.12.50 – 2.9.74	Formed from part of 226 OCU with 7 x T.7s plus other types. Became Hunter OCU. Became TWU from 2.9.74 (a few Meteors still in use). Meteors coded ES until 3.53
231 OCU	T.7, FR.9, PR.10	1.12.51 – 15.12.90	Reformed 1.12.51. Absorbed 237 OCU on same day. A Canberra unit primarily, ex-237 OCU Meteors used to 1956
233 OCU	T.7, F.8	1.9.52 – 1.9.57	Provided operational fighter training for Hunter pilots. Meteors used in support roles only.
237 OCU	T.7, FR.9, PR.10	31.7.47 – 1.12.51	Formed as 237 (PR) OCU with PR Mosquitoes and Spitfires. Meteors rec'd later. Merged with 231 OCU. Code LP
238 OCU	NF.11, 12, NF.14, T.7*, F.8*	15.6.52 – 17.3.58	OCU training night fighter radar operators. Meteors rec'd later. To North Luffenham 1.1.57 where it absorbed the All Weather & Night Fighter OCU (AW&NFOCU)
All Weather & NF OCU	T.7, F.8, NF.12, 14	1.4.55 – 1.1.57	Formed at North Luffenham. Disbanded into 238 OCU
1 ANS	T.7, NF(T).14	15.3.57 – 26.8.70	Reformed 3.57. Meteors used 1962 to 2.66 (1 x T.7, 10 or 12 x NF(T).14). DB and absorbed by 6 FTS
2 ANS	T.7, NF(T).14	4.6.47 – 1.5.70	Meteors used 6.1959 to 1962 (transferred to 1 ANS)
TWU	T.7, F.8	2.9.74 – 31.8.92	Formed from 229 0CU. Became 1 TWU when 2 TWU formed 31.7.78. Unit operated two of the RAF's last Meteors: VZ467 & WA669. Both gone by 22.10.82 and stored. WA669 later joined CFS for 'Vintage Pair' c 1985
3/4 CAACU	T.7, TT.20	1.7.54 – 31.12.71	Formed 7.54 by amalgamating 3 CAACU and 4 CAACU at Exeter. First TT.20 received 16.1.1962
5 CAACU	F.4, T.7, F.8, TT.20	16.9.51 – 30.9.71	Believed to have operated Meteors from c 1957 with TT.20s from 1962 onwards
RAE Llanbedr	T.7, U.15, D.16, NF.14, TT.20	1954 – 2004	Used for air-to-air guided missile evaluation against unmanned target aircraft. Llanbedr's last operating Meteor, D.16 WK800, was retired intact in 2004

Note: Unit codes are included only if known with some degree of accuracy;   * Used in a support role.

■ APPENDIX 5 **ROYAL NAVY METEOR SQUADRONS**

Squadron	Mark(s)	Period used	Comments
700 Squadron	TT.20	12.59 – 7.61	
700 Z Squadron	T.7	5.61 – 11.61	
702 Squadron	T.7	6.49 – 8.52	
703 Squadron	T.7 F.3, F.8	7.50 – 8.55 (T.7)	F.3s were EE337 (made first British twin-jet carrier landing on 8.6.48) & EE387. F.8 was WK942 *c* 5.53.
728 Squadron	T.7, TT.20	2.55 – 5.67 (T.7) 3.58 – 5.67	TT.20s replaced Sturgeon TT.3s at Hal Far, Malta
728(B) Squadron	U.15 U.16 (D.16)	7.59 – 10.61 10.60 – 11.61	Targets for Seaslug SAMs fired by HMS *Girdle Ness* (Firefly U.9s & Canberra D.14s used concurrently)
736 Squadron	T.7	8.52 – 5.54	
759 Squadron	T.7	9.52 – 4.54	
764 Squadron	T.7	12.57 – 2.57	
767 Squadron	T.7	2.53 – 12.53	
771 Squadron	T.7	5.50 – 3.55	
778 Squadron	F.3	?	EE337 *might* have been briefly allocated to the Squadron following its reconditioning *c* 1952.
781 Squadron	T.7	4.51 – 6.54	
806 Squadron	T.7	3.53 – 4.53	
813 Squadron	T.7	3.53 – 12.53	

Some other RN Meteor users

Several RN station flights received at least one Meteor T.7 with examples allocated to Brawdy, Ford, Hal Far, Lossiemouth, Stretton and Yeovilton amongst others – to which Brawdy added TT.20, WD585 briefly in 12.59. Mention must be made of Airwork Ltd, a civilian-run unit which commenced work in 1.50, at Brawdy, to provide aircraft for cooperation with RN units. They also operated jet conversion courses using T.7s (among other types). In 1.61 the unit moved to Yeovilton where it operated as the Air Direction Training Unit until merging into the Fleet Requirements and Air Direction Unit (FRADU) on 1.12.72. The same company also established the Airwork Fleet Requirements Unit (FRU) at Hurn on 1.9.52 which eventually came to provide all the RN's FRU needs using a host of aircraft types over the years. The FRU moved to Yeovilton in October 1972 and it too became a component of FRADU. Meteor TT.20s were used by the FRU from 5.58 to 3.71 with T.7s in use until 3.71 also.

■ APPENDIX 6 BRITISH METEOR SERIAL ALLOCATIONS

The following list records the serial ranges assigned to Meteors intended for use by Britain (RAF, RN, MoS etc.) It is misleading in that it includes several airframes which, having received British serial numbers, were then held for transfer or sale abroad, most *prior* to being issued to RAF or FAA units excepting, presumably, maintenance or storage units. Consequently, it remains unclear as to precisely how many Meteors entered British service. One example might suffice to illustrate the point: of the seven Meteors allocated serials commencing X (XF273-XF279), one went to Boscombe Down (XF274), one to Belgium (XF273), while the remainder went to the Netherlands. The practise shouldn't come as surprise though given Britain's parlous economic state in the post-war years when additional export orders were much welcomed – as indeed they still are!

Gloster F.9/40

DG202-DG209

Meteor F.1

EE210-EE229

Meteor F.2

DG207 became F.2 prototype

Meteor F.3

EE230-EE254, EE269-EE318, EE331-EE369, EE384-EE429, EE444-EE493

Meteor F.4

EE517-EE554, EE568-EE599, RA365-RA398, RA413-RA457, RA473-RA493, VT102-VT150, VT168-VT199, VT213-VT247, VT256-VT294, VT303-VT347, VW255-VW304, VW308-VW317, VW780-VW791, VZ386-VZ429, VZ436, VZ437. (Also F.3, EE360, converted to F.4 prototype and Gloster's civil registered Mk.4, G-AIDC. Approximately eighty-six F.4s were allocated to other countries from amongst these serials).

Meteor F.5

VT347 – (ex-F.4)

Meteor T.7

VW410-VW459, VW470-VW489, VZ629-VZ649, WA590-WA639, WA649-WA698, WA707-WA743, WF766-WF795, WF813-WF862, WF875-WF883, WG935-WG950, WG961-WG999, WH112-WH136, WH164-WH209, WH215-WH248, WL332-WL381, WL397-WL436, WL453-WL488, WN309-WN321, WS103-WS117, WS140-WS151, XF273-XF279. (Also, Gloster's civil registered G-AKPK [rebuilt from G-AIDC], G-ANSO [rebuilt from modified Mk.8 G-7-1] and F.4 rebuilds EE530 and EE573. Approximately 101 x T.7s were allocated to other countries from amongst these serials).

Meteor F.8

VZ438-VZ485, VZ493-VZ532, VZ540-VZ569, WA755-WA794, WA808-WA857, WA867-WA909, WA920-WA969, WA981-WA999, WB105-WB112, WE852-WE891, WE895-WE939, WE942-WE976, WF639-WF662, WF677-WF716, WF736-WF760, WH249-WH263, WH272-WH320, WH342-WH386, WH395-WH426, WH442-WH484, WH498-WH513, WK647-WK696, WK707-WK756, WK783-WK827, WK849-WK893, WK906-WK955, WK966-WK994, WL104-WL143, WL158-WL191. (Also F.4, VT150, became F.8 prototype, and Gloster Private Venture/Ground Attack Fighter, G-AMCJ, [later G-7-1 then G-ANSO]. Approximately 146 x F.8s were allocated to other countries from these serials. An additional five, possibly more, were converted to U.21A drones for Australia.)

Meteor FR.9

VW360-VW371, VZ577-VZ611, WB113-WB125, WB133-WB143, WH533-WH557, WL255-WL265, WX962-WX981. (Twenty-one FR.9s were allocated to other countries from amongst these serials).

Meteor PR.10

VS968-VS987, VW376-VW379, VZ620, WB153-WB181, WH569-WH573

Meteor NF.11

WA546, WA547, WB543, WD585-WD634, WD640-WD689, WD696-WD745, WD751-WD800, WM143-WM192, WM221-WM270, WM292-WM307, WM368-WM403. (Plus T.7, VW413, which became the NF.11 prototype. At least eighty-six NF.11s, perhaps slightly, more were allocated to other countries from within these serials – forty-one went to France).

Meteor NF.12

WS590-WS639, WS658-WS700, WS715-WS721. (Plus, NF.11, WD687, which became the NF.12 prototype).

Meteor NF.13

WM308-WM341, WM362-WM367. (About twenty NF.13s were allocated to other countries from these serials, either directly from the production line or via later transfers).

Meteor NF.14

WS722-WS760, WS744-WS812, WS827-WS848. (Also, NF.11, WM261, which became NF.14 prototype. Two NF.14s were allocated to other countries from these serials).

■ APPENDIX 7 **METEOR BASIC DATA**

	Powerplant	Max speed in 'clean' condition	Span	Length	Ceiling
F.1 (DG202 similar)	RR Welland 1	411mph (661kph) at S/L 445mph (716kph) at 30,000ft (9,144m)	43ft 0in (13.106m)	41ft 5in (12.623m)	43,000ft (13,106m)
F.2	DH H.1 Goblin	? at S/L 505mph (813kph) at 30,000ft (9,144m)	44ft 3in (13.487m)	41ft 5in (12.623m)	49,000ft (14,935m)
F.3	RR Welland 1 RR Derwent 1	? at S/L 485mph (780kph) at S/L 493mph (793kph) at 30,000ft (9,144m)	43ft 0in (13.106m)	41ft 5in (12.623m)	46,000ft (14,020m)
F.4	RR Derwent 5	585mph (937kph) at S/L 550mph (885kph) at 30,000ft (9,144m)	43ft 0in (13.106m)	41ft 0in (12.496m)	45,000ft (13,716m)
F.4 'clip-wing'	RR Derwent 5	590mph at S/L (950kph)	37ft 2in (11.328m)	41ft 0in (12.496m)	44,300ft (13,502m)
T.7	RR Derwent 5 RR Derwent 8	– 585mph (937kph) at S/L 540mph (869kph) at 30,000ft (9,144m)	37ft 2in (11.328m)	43ft 6in (13.258m)	45,000ft (13,716m)
F.8	RR Derwent 8	592mph (953kph) at S/L 553mph (890kph) at 30,000ft (9,144m)	37ft 2in (11.328m)	44ft 7in (13.589m)	44,000ft (13,411m)
FR.9	RR Derwent 8	593mph (954kph) at S/L 553mph (890kph) at 30,000ft (9,144m)	37ft 2in (11.328m)	45ft 4in * (13.817m)	44,000ft (13,411m)
PR.10	RR Derwent 8	? at S/L 575mph (925kph) at 10,000ft (9,144m)	43ft 0in (13.106m)	44ft 3in (13.487m)	47,300ft (14,417m)
NF.11	RR Derwent 8	580mph (933kph) at S/L 546mph (879kph) (30,000ft (9,144m)	43ft 0in (13.106m)	48ft 6in (14.782m)	40,000ft (12,192m)
NF.12	RR Derwent 9	? at S/L 580mph (933kph) at 10,000ft (3,048m)	43ft 0in (13.106m)	49ft 11in (15.214m)	40,000ft (12,192m)
NF.13	RR Derwent 8	? at S/L 580mph (933kph) at 10,000ft (3,048m)	43ft 0in (13.106m)	48ft 6in (14.782m)	c 39,000ft (11,887m)
NF.14	RR Derwent 9	? at S/L 585mph (941kph) at 10,000ft (3,048m)	43ft 0in (13.106m)	49ft 11in† (15.214m)	c 42,000ft (12,801m)

* The FR.9's camera installation increased fuselage length by 9in. Most sources incorrectly quote a length of 44ft 7in – the same as the F.8 (Courtesy John Adams);   † Fuselage length was reduced by 3½ inches if a tail warning radar was fitted in lieu of the original tail cone.

Other than the unarmed T.7 and PR.10 all RAF frontline Meteor variants carried four 20mm Hispano Mk 5 cannon in the nose (day fighters) or wings (night fighters). The F.3, F.4, F.8 and FR.9 could carry bombs, while both the F.8 and FR.9 could accommodate single or double-tier RPs if required.

■ APPENDIX 8 **GLOSSARY**

A&AEE Aircraft & Armament Experimental Establishment
AFDS Air Fighting Development Squadron
AES Air Electronics School
AFS Advanced Flying School
AHU Aircraft Holding Unit
AI Air Intercept (radar)
ANS Air Navigation School
APC Armament Practice Camp
APS Armament Practice Station
AW&NF All Weather & Night Fighter
BAC British Aircraft Corporation
BCCS Bomber Command Communication Squadron
CAACU Civilian Anti-Aircraft Co-operation Unit
CATCS Central Air Traffic Control School
CF Communication Flight; often prefixed with location e.g. Aden CF
CFE Central Fighter Establishment
CFS Central Flying School
CGS Central Gunnery School
CNCS Central Navigation & Control School

CS Communication Squadron; often prefixed with location e.g. Aden CS
CSDE Central Servicing Development Establishment
CSE Central Signals Establishment
CU Conversion Unit
DB Disbanded
DFCS Day Fighter Combat Squadron
DFLS Day Fighter Leaders School
ECM Electronic Counter Measures
ETPS Empire Test Pilots School
FCS Fighter Combat School (a component of the CFE)
FCIRS Fighter Command Instrument Rating Squadron
FRADU Fleet Requirements & Air Direction Unit
FRL Flight Refuelling Ltd
FTS Flying Training School
GAC Gloster Aircraft Company
HSS High Speed Silver
IFR In-flight refuelling
MoA Ministry of Aviation

MoD(PE) Ministry of Defence (Procurement Executive)
MoS Ministry of Supply
MU Maintenance Unit
NEA Non-effective airframe
OCU Operational Conversion Unit
RAE Royal Aircraft Establishment (Royal Aerospace Establishment from 1st April 1988)
RauxAF Royal Auxiliary Air Force
RAFC Royal Air Force College
RAFCAW RAF College of Air Warfare
RAFFC Royal Air Force Flying College
RRE Radar Research Establishment
SOC Struck Off Charge
SoTT School of Technical Training
TACAN TACtical Air Navigation
TAF Tactical Air Force (e.g. 2TAF)
THum Flt Temperature and HUMidity Flight
TRE Telecommunications Research Establishment
TT Target Tug
TWU Tactical Weapons Unit